SAINTS
— OF THE —
SOUTH WEST

James Mildren

BOSSINEY BOOKS

Gunwalloe Church

First published in 1989 by
Bossiney Books
St Teath, Bodmin, Cornwall.

Typeset and Printed by
Clowes Book Printers
St Columb, Cornwall.

Front cover: St Michael's
Mount
Back cover: St Just in Roseland
Church

PLATE ACKNOWLEDGMENTS
Cover photography by Ray
Bishop
Alice Boyd: pages 29, 38, 41,
52, 53, 58, 68, 82, 86, 93
Felicity Young: pages 6, 11, 24,
27, 45, 57, 73, back cover
Ray Bishop: pages 12, 19, 32,
43, 47, 77, 85, 95
Woolf-Greenham: pages 31, 64
Devon Library Services: page
71

About the Author and the Book

This is James Mildren's fourth title for Bossiney: *Dartmoor in the Old Days* and *Castles of Devon*, both still in print, and *125 Years with The Western Morning News* were all warmly received – and remain valuable contributions to the Westcountry library. Here he opens our 1989 programme with *Saints of the South West.*

James Mildren is an occasional radio broadcaster. He edited the script of Television South West's *Hurried Into Eternity,* and wrote and presented the award-winning *Road to Trenarren,* an appreciation of A. L. Rowse's poetry. In 1988 Plymouth City commissioned him to write the best-selling *The Incredible Armada* which resulted in numerous radio and TV appearances. He also wrote the script read by Sir Michael Horden, and helped devise the historic Grand Finale night Armada 400 celebrations on Plymouth Hoe. He retired from full-time journalism in July 1988 to devote himself to writing books.

James Mildren

Introducing Saints
of the Southwest

The volumes about the Saints, written by such authorities as Canon
Doble and the Reverend Sabine Baring-Gould, look ominously dusty
on the library shelves today but they contain a treasure trove about
those great missionaries who devoted their lives to Jesus Christ and
His teachings.

They combined vigour with virtue and, through them, close ties
were established between the people of the Westcountry and Brittany
– ties which have been neglected until recent times.

In writing this small work, I was always conscious of being on the
edge of the quicksands of which the great Devon historian, Dr W. G.
Hoskins had warned all those daring to follow the historic trail.
Sometimes, I fear, I may have tumbled in!

But this has been an adventure into the remote past of Cornwall
and Devon helping me, as I hope it may help others, to put into
perspective the seeming self-preoccupation of our own disordered
age. The Saints still have a message for us all and I am moved to
dedicate this book to the memory of St Brigid, for her humour, and to
the angelic and lovably humble St Winwaloe, who understood so
well, it seems, the frailties of our 'cumbering frames of clay.'

James Mildren
Devonport, 1988

Saints of the South West

For almost 1,000 years no foreign invader has sullied British soil. The same cannot, however, be said for the previous millennium.

Even before Caesar's first excursions across the Channel and, a century later, the conquest of Britain by the Emperor Claudius' legions, a wave of warrior tribes had washed across these relatively warm and fertile shores.

The Celts had swarmed over much of Europe in the six centuries before Christ. These tall, fair-headed men and women intermingled with the short, dark Iberian stock in a land where, at the time, the untamed forest was lord.

Of their religious beliefs we know little. But the deep, dark interiors of those extensive woodlands, which environmentalists of our own age would surely have venerated, were the subject of mystery and worship 2,000 years ago.

Local deities haunted those moist and mossy floors beneath the shadowy green canopy; monsters and serpents lurked in caverns; spirits dwelt beneath cold, wet springs and wells; the fearsome, roaring winds whipping the clouds up and down the mountainsides inspired awe, and bred superstition in the minds of these people. It was no uphill task for the Druid priesthood to invest perplexing Nature with an air of the occult or to inculcate terror in all hearts. Its ministry was such that even the patrician Caesar was shocked: the Romans made up their minds to eliminate it. There was, however, another factor illuminating history's stage, nothing less than the birth of Jesus Christ.

If all that seems so very long ago, then let us bring our thoughts forward to the present. In British history, three dates stand out – Caesar's invasion of 55 BC, the Norman Conquest of 1066, and the defeat of the Spanish Armada in 1588.

Over the huge timescape of the last 2,000 years those events occurred at the beginning, the half-way and the three-quarter stage in our history. But what of the missing quarter stage? Of the period around 450 to 600 AD – the dawn of the so-called Dark Ages? It would be satisfying to be able to insert a victory of King Arthur's – but whether he was real, or imaginary, we do not know for certain. With the withdrawal of the Romans from Britain, around 407 AD, a great darkness steals over our history.

That period is seemingly inexorable in its profound silence, broken, momentarily, by the march of the exalted St Augustine of Canterbury and his monks through these islands, and the subsequent return of the Latin alphabet and the written record. If Augustine failed to find God in Nature, he had ample testament that it had been created by Him. Yet Augustine's great mission was to evangelize Anglo-Saxon England, to transform those Angles into Angels. He arrived in 597.

What, however, is so often overlooked by historians is that the Christian ministry, so abhorred by the Nordic Anglo-Saxons, had spread steadily through the, as yet, unconquered and isolated western provinces of Britain.

The Anglo-Saxon onrush, held up for a couple of centuries while the Roman custodians were in evidence, crushed everything in its path from around 428 onwards. But not until 577 with their victories at Dyrham, north of Bath, and, in 613, near the Roman ruins of Chester, did they finally manage to segregate the Celts into pockets of resistance in Wales, Devon and Cornwall and Strathclyde. The heathen invaders failed, notably, to subjugate Devon and Cornwall until much later, and it was in these counties, known as Dumnonia, between the years 450 and 600 approximately, that a most remarkable chain of events was to occur.

The period has become known generally as *The Age of the Saints.* Little of written historical record remains of the period. Most has been lost. But archaeological exploration is slowly uncovering and corroborating evidence of an astonishing period in the Westcountry's past. Of holy men and women who, though hemmed in by pagan swarms, carried the divine and glorious message of the resurrected

Over land such as this The Saints may have travelled carrying the message 'of the resurrected Christ to the Celtic people.'

Christ to the Celtic people. Heralds of Light. They combined, in seeming never-ending abundance, virtue with virility.

And, so often overlooked by national historians, this Christian faith was flourishing among the Celts long before the great Pope Gregory despatched St Augustine to convert the heathen English. The wondrous story of the Celtic Saints involves seeming miracles and a mysterious plague. It interweaves natural with supernatural, tells of friends and deadly enemies, and exemplifies the gruesome and the glorious in humankind.

But let us begin our tale at Exeter Cathedral with Bishop John Grandisson in the year 1330.

Grandisson wrote to the Archdeacon of Cornwall complaining that many of the records of local Cornish Saints appeared to have been lost, or destroyed. Grandisson seemed determined to compile a complete list, and he followed up his criticism by instructing parish priests, on penalty of a fine, to make copies of all the surviving records in their care. The Bishop may have been conscious of the contribution made by a monk, John of Tynemouth who, in the first half of the century, made an extensive tour of England recording the names of Saints, and the details of their lives, for his Martyrologium and Sanctilogium.

Unfortunately, John of Tynemouth did not visit Exeter, and neglected to make any mention of the Saints of Devon and Cornwall. Grandisson sought to repair the omission. But when, in 1366, he drew up his Legendarium for use in the Cathedral, he chose to ignore all the Celtic Saints except St Melor and St Samson. Worse still, the material which he collected from the parish priests is now lost.

Fortunately, however, the relationship between Cornwall and Brittany was exceptionally close, closer even than that with Ireland or Wales. The Saxon scourge had bound them together. This Nordic invasion had driven many of the Romanised Celts, a number of whom might well have inherited a Christian tradition, to seek a new life in the western fringes of Britain. They fled into Wales, Devon and Cornwall, and from there to the relative safety of Armorica, as Brittany was known until the sixth century. Indeed, Cornish settlements in this remote region of France were so numerous that the Southwest portion of Armorica between the Elorn and the Ellé became known as Cornouaille after Cornwall, and Armorica itself as Lesser Britain or Britannia, according to Gregory of Tours.

That fiercely independent region, harmoniously bound then by ties of a more or less common language and religion with the Cornish, proved troublesome in the kingdom of France up to and beyond the time of the French Revolution itself. It held fast to the traditions of a dim and distant past.

But if the people of Cornwall and Cornouaille were interchangeable, then so were their Saints. What Grandisson and John of Tynemouth had failed to preserve, the Breton scribes, mercifully, remembered and recorded. Even today, we see in the place-names and parishes of Brittany and Cornwall, the extraordinary parallels created by these early Christian martyrs. It is through the names of towns and villages, no mere coincidence, that these great Heralds of Light left their most permanent and indelible memorials in the Lands of the Saints.

Ingrained in the names of dozens of Westcountry communities and, no less, in those up and down the Breton peninsula, the Saints are invoked, celebrated and commemorated. Suddenly, through these very place names, the fabric of time is ripped asunder, and we are enabled to peer faintly down a stairwell into the shadowy recesses of the Dark Ages themselves.

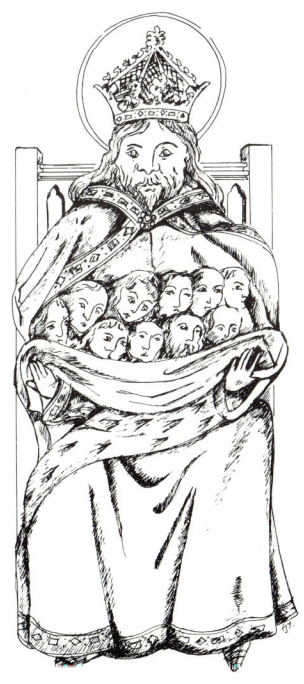

King Brychan of Wales, the father of twelve men and twelve women all of whom became Saints or Martyrs. And it was almost certainly as a result of his children's activities that the old saying 'There are more Saints in Cornwall than in Heaven' came about.

The Cornish academic, William Copeland Borlase, wrote 'There seems little ground for hope that we shall ever be able to gain a perfectly true insight into the history of this epoch, or to unravel the meshes of so tangled a web.'

But the writer, Sir Arthur Quiller-Couch, scorned such a philosophy of hopelessness. It was as if Borlase, said Q, felt his task similar to gathering up broken pieces of pottery from some ancient tomb, in the hope of fitting them together and making one large and perfect vase, but finding during the process that they belonged to several vessels, none of which were capable of restoration as a whole. 'Though', he added, 'some faint notion of the pristine shape of each may be gathered from the general pattern and contour of its shards.'

Is it, then, to the historian of imagination rather than the probing archaeologist that the Saints are likelier to give up their secrets? All that can be gained from the materials at hand is a reasonable probability, wrote Borlase, that Cornwall, before it bent its neck to the See of Canterbury, had been invaded by three distinct streams of missionary effort – from Ireland, from Wales, from Brittany. But in what order they came, no-one can say, for certain. Borlase was precise, and correct, but even he would have to admit that the place names are of an indisputable sincerity.

'The thought of Celtic Saints, wandering the shores of Devon, or meditating in their little oratories, in primeval woods, seduces the imagination', wrote the percipient Devon historian, Dr W. G. Hoskins. 'Whoever approaches the Celtic Saints walks on the edge of a quicksand, but a quicksand concealing valuable treasure.' That treasure has been sought out, for all the quaking mire into which it has slithered, by many fine writers – explorers of the human condition.

Sabine Baring-Gould (1834-1924), the Victorian squire-parson of

'The thought of Celtic Saints, wandering the shores of Devon, or meditating in their little oratories, in primeval woods, seduces the imagination' wrote Devon historian Dr W G Hoskins.

Sabine Baring-Gould the Victorian squire-parson of Lewtrenchard.

Lewtrenchard, dedicated his four-volume work which was compiled jointly with John Fisher, to a quartet of pioneers in Celtic hagiography, the study of Saints – the Reverend Rice-Rees, Albert Le Grand, John Colgan and the recusant Cornishman, Nicholas Roscarrock (1549-1633). The Catholic Roscarrock, who narrowly escaped martyrdom for practising his outlawed faith in Elizabethan England, compiled a catalogue of the Saints of Great Britain. A fascinating work from a man who had good cause to fear every knock at his door.

Richard Carew (1555-1620) of Antony could scarcely ignore the Cornish Saints in his Survey, nor did a great and much lamented fellow Cornishman, Charles Henderson, in our own century. Happily, Henderson was able to combine much of his talent with the most outstanding hagiographer of them all – Canon Gilbert Hunter Doble (1880-1945), Vicar of Wendron, and the supreme student of the Celtic Saints of Cornwall. The good vicar was not always especially charitably disposed when dealing with the errors to be found in his fellow clergyman's earlier work written at Lewtrenchard. Yet Doble, like Baring-Gould, had little or no fear of the historical quicksands.

'The fact that a parish or village or farm or well is called after a Saint is sometimes proof that he lived there, or that it afterwards belonged to his monastery and that monks from his monastery visited it, or that some of the Saint's relics were at a later period given to the church there,' wrote Doble, whose wonderful word-pictures conjure up the very essence of the period – from the tonsure, which was the shaving of the head, to the sacrifices and self-denial each Saint voluntarily undertook.

He presents, for example, a portrait of St Budoc, said to have been a great teacher, who often stayed at Budock Vean. The Saint also lent his name to the now crowded Plymouth suburbs of St Budeaux and Budshead, beside the sequestered creek at Tamerton Foliot on the River Tamar. Budoc's monastery was typical of its time – a cluster of beehive huts – not the analogy of the holy cells with that of the tireless honey-gatherers – surrounded by an enclosure. At the heart was a small church built of wood and stone, with a well nearby, and a great stone cross. Budoc was earnest and cultured, as befitted a teacher. There was, perhaps, a degree of the pedagogue about him – virtuous but maybe not quite as virile as the young monks who listened.

However, Doble tells us, the Saint was liable to discipline himself – doubtless from the lusts and temptations of the flesh – by immersing himself up to his neck in the cold waters of the Helford River reciting psalms all the while. We shall learn how two other great Celtic Saints met in like fashion. At his side, Budoc wore a wallet containing a beautifully-inscribed psalter – the imaginative Celts were superb artists. In one hand he carried a short staff, with spade-like head; in the other, a large bell also, doubtless, marvellously decorated and inscribed.

15

What would instantly strike the modern onlooker would have been Budoc's tonsure. The front of his head was shaven from ear to ear. It earned these men the derisive title of Adze-head! Their long faces and curved, bald pates, bore such a striking resemblance to the tool with which they worked the land. Yet that distinctive tonsure was an unmistakably characteristic mark of the Celtic monk.

St Budoc and his brothers, some, but not all of whom would have been fully-fledged ordained priests, would have spent much of their time cultivating the glebe land around their monastery. Those hours not taken up with prayer would have been devoted to reading or copying books. Their rule was a very strict one – to 'keep under' their bodies with fasting, and privation.

Years earlier, Budoc had first arrived at this place – long before the monastery was created. For 40 days and 40 nights he fasted. That was the key to possession of the land. It was an ancient right, entitling the holy man to take occupancy, and to seek out those of a like mind to help him create a consecrated, holy place on that site. Once established, the missionary might move on, leaving charge of the monastery which he had founded, and which now bore his name, to a devoted follower. He would then seek out another site to sanctify, and spread the Gospel further among the heathen people. On the Tamar, perhaps, in St Budoc's case – or by ship across Falmouth Bay to Brittany.

Nothing became a monk so much as his three obligations: obedience, chastity and poverty. The monk's outward show of holy estate was a white tunic, with cowl. In cold weather, a mantle – amphibalus, sometimes called chasuble – was thrown protectively over the shoulders. But many, we learn, delighted in clothing themselves in the skins of goat, sheep or fawn. Clothing which was a far cry from the ecclesiastical sartorial elegance of later ages. Yet their outstanding characteristic, it would seem, was their wholly immoderate fasting and self-torture – again, so distant in time and habit from their successors in the later Middle Ages whose immodesty was to rent the Church in twain.

The Keys of the Kingdom were in the hearts of these simple but singularly-minded Celts of long ago. Their followers were dedicated and devoted. Certain as they were of Heaven, then, equally their Saintly piety could turn to vengeance, and curses of endless woe against those who dared defy or offend them. For it was the duty of the Saint to denounce the enemies of his tribal chieftain. Baring-Gould tells us that it was held that a curse once launched could not be recalled: if it did not strike, it recoiled upon the Saint or bard who had pronounced it.

It is clear from the Welsh legends that the Saints took such duties seriously – as did the tribal leaders, especially before battle. The nature of these curses is unknown, but the strictures of these holy men, delivered, perhaps, from a mountainside, calling down the damnation of the Almighty upon their foes, was clearly intended to strike fear into the hearts of all within hearing distance. There is no shortage of mighty texts from Biblical sources.

The Saints also used fasting as a weapon against their enemies. It is an age-old means of retaliation. It is said, for example, that St Keverne went seven years without sleep – that he held up his arm until it became so rigid that a bird laid and hatched her eggs in the palm of his hand!

Baring-Gould also argues that because of the endemic poverty which existed, the Saints of Ireland were prone to pray to the Almighty 'to reduce the number of the lower class that the rest might live in comfort.' The Yellow Plague followed, he said. But to keep the population in balance the choice of alternative evils amounted to war, migration or compulsory celibacy. Hardly any wonder, perhaps, that the holy men of Ireland prayed for Divine intervention, though the Yellow Plague, had this really been the Almighty's answer, made no distinction between pauper and priest.

The Yellow Plague, probably some deadly form of hepatitis, broke out in the year 547. Its origins are curious. It was said to have been preceded by the appearance of a vaporous column sweeping over the land with one end in the clouds and the other trailing along the ground. Some sources suggest that this watery column discharged heavy rain in its wake. All who came within its path sickened to death. It was said to have affected not only men, but also their animals.

This Pesta Flava, as it was known, responded to no medicine, and raged for a period of five years in Britain and Europe. Its ravages were such that it well-nigh depopulated the areas chiefly affected – and was clearly both a personal affliction and a social calamity. The vector for this disease is very much a mystery; dogs, rats? We may never know.

But it would seem that it was not a pestilence of the bubonic variety, since there is uniformity of evidence that it took its name from the yellow and bloodless appearance of those afflicted. It has been postulated that the Yellow Plague spread across Europe from the Middle East during the five years before 547.

The Yellow Plague occurred during the lifetime of one of the best-known and most influential of Welsh Saints, St Teilo, a friend of St David. And it is from his life story that we learn of the pestilence, and the vaporous column in the sky with which it was associated. When the plague came, St Teilo fled into Cornwall, where he was received amicably by King Geraint.

From Cornwall, St Teilo, almost certainly still in flight from the danger of the Yellow Plague, travelled on to Brittany, and to St Samson at Dol. He spent his time there helping his brother Saint in laying out the monastery orchard, and we are told that he remained in Armorica from 548 until 556. He recrossed into Cornwall, arriving at Falmouth, and travelled on to a place called Dingerein which, 'was now marked by mounds, the palace of Geraint, the King, who was dying.' We shall return, later, to Dingerein, and the possibility that this Din (fort) of Gerein (Geraint) may have been none other than Tintagel.

St Teilo's life is, of course, hedged around with miracles as well as historical facts. A story is told that he had forseen the death of Geraint, and set adrift from Brittany, a stone sarcophagus, which floated over to Cornwall, and served for the King's interment. And St Teilo, it is little surprise to learn, was no slouch when it came to cursing his enemies. In 577, after the great battle of Dyrham, and the victory of the Anglo-Saxons, the victorious heathen crossed the River Wye. It was St Teilo who stood by his King to bless his forces and to curse the enemy. Somewhat ironically, Teilo, when asked: 'What is the greatest wisdom in a man,' is said to have replied, 'To refrain from injuring another when he has the power to do so.'

But the Saints had other duties to the community, such as the education of the young, to conduct worship and to bury the dead. Burial from late Roman times onwards was an extended inhumation, with the head laid to the west, so that the Christian might rise up, on the Day of Judgement, facing east.

The Celtic Saints, though their methods may sometimes seem unsophisticated, not to say crude, were devoted Christians. The principal gathering was on Sundays for the Lord's Supper. Baptism

The sea was an important link between Cornwall and Brittany with many of the Saints crossing and re-crossing it in their missions as Heralds of Light.

was by complete immersion in the healing waters, and the services were conducted in Latin. The Saints, revered for their learning, preached the Gospel and ministered to the people.

Revered, also, was the memory of their deeds and, in time, the title of Saint was attached to their name, though this had nothing to do with formal canonization, as we now understand that word. It is derived, quite simply from the Latin, Sanctus, meaning Holy, which, in itself, originates from the old English word meaning whole, or healthy. The faith was essentially Christian. They worshipped God in the simplicity and the beauty of holiness. Not in grand cathedrals, but in rough-hewn stone huts thatched over with whatever material was available.

The monks lived as hermits in the little cells surrounding the central church building, and provided a strong and shining example of austerity. The monasteries were little more than congeries of detached stone or wooden huts. Two good examples have survived – at Perranzabuloe and at Tintagel – and each has its story to tell, one from the past, the other, hopefully, for the future!

It was St Piran who was said to have founded the little church at Perranzabuloe, when he came to Cornwall in 490. Before we discuss the little oratory which he built in the sand, it is worth examining what is known about the Patron Saint of Cornwall himself. As we know, Celtic Saints were not canonized in the formal sense of the word, they were venerated and loved founders of monastic settlements. Piran, it is said, floated to Cornwall from Ireland on a millstone – but then, both St Crantock and St Petroc came across on their altar-stones, and St Kea in a stone trough.

There is probably a very simple explanation for these 'miracle' voyages. Perranzabuloe, under Piran's leadership and guidance, grew into a monastery of some importance, and Piran was a Saint who clearly believed that good could emanate from commercial application. He is said to have made a collection of Cornish rocks, with their high mineral content. His fireplace was made of a single stone, 'black as coals', and when it became very hot, he was surprised to discover a stream of white metal trickling on to the hearth. It was tin, of course, and Piran's emblem, the Cornish flag, is a white cross on a black background.

The oratory at Perranzabuloe was created in the sixth century and, in 1873, the Bishop of Truro, the scholarly Dr Benson, described it as 'The oldest sanctuary in the land except, perhaps, St Martin's Church at Canterbury.' But in the sixteenth century, the parish of Perranzabuloe was 'almost drowned with the sea-sand that the North West wind whirleth and driveth to the land, in such sort as the inhabitants have already been forced to remove their church: they daily lose their land.' The historian Carew noted: 'Where the sand meeteth with any crossing brook, the same by a secret antipathy restraineth and barreth his farther encroaching that way.'

Near the Perran Oratory there once existed a lake, called the

Vlow, and the sand never blew across it. But a miner called Roberts, or Robartes – perhaps an ancestor of the Robartes who built Lanhydrock House, Bodmin, and afforded the cost from his profits at mining – drove in an adit towards a mine and drained the water from the lake. Thus, after 1,000 years, one of the treasures of Cornwall was obliterated by sand.

In the early part of the nineteenth century an old man called Jenkin found the walls of the oratory showing above the sand and correctly deduced this was the lost church of tradition. In September, 1835, it was excavated by William Michell of Truro. He found that many bodies were interred both in the chancel and nave of the tiny oratory. The skeletons were two feet below the floors, and of the three with their feet underlying the altar, one was said to have been of a man who, in life, would have been seven feet six inches tall – now headless.

In the ancient burial ground to the west were found hundreds of skeletons, all laid east and west and some with crossed legs – 'like those of the Knights Templar'. The external dimensions of the Oratory (the walls were two feet in thickness) were given as 29 feet 6 inches in length and 16 feet 6 inches in width. The gables were 19 feet in height. Could it be that St Piran was buried here, as tradition states, with his mother? His head, it should be noted, was said to have been carried to the daughter church of St Agnes.

In 1281, an inventory was made at the church of St Piran – which had superceded the oratory – which recorded 'and a box in which was kept St Piran's head' and in 1433, Sir John Arundell, knight, bequeathed 40 shillings to the parish 'to enclose the Saint's head honourably.' The head, the Saint's pectoral staff, his silver cross and his bell of copper were said to have been conveyed to the second church early in the twelfth century, and his shrine was maintained until 1559. It is probable that either the purges of the Reformation or the vandalism of the Puritans put paid to that.

The little oratory in the sands was again covered by the late nineteenth century, and the ruins were enclosed by railings. But these were vandalised by tourists, who plainly professed more in the way of ignorance than courtesy towards Cornish customs. In 1910, the ancient building was covered with protective concrete in an endeavour to save it from its three enemies – sand, water and vandals.

But it could not survive. By the 1950s, the concrete roof had become dangerous, and the drain laid in 1910, in an effort to clear off some of the water, had become buried beneath 15 feet of sand. Efforts were made to restore the drain, but it collapsed once again. Meantime vandals played football on the sanctuary floor, using the altar as goalposts. They destroyed a great wooden cross, broke perspex lights, and scrawled graffiti over the walls.

Inside, the water level built up: in 1974, the Fire Brigade pumped out 250,000 gallons, but the level dropped a mere one and a half inches. Today, it has been decently buried again, beneath the sands, to lie in wait, perhaps, until some great storm of the future reveals once again Cornwall's national shrine to a less indifferent public.

I well remember visiting it while on holiday at Perranporth in 1974, and wrote as follows in my diary: 'Walked across the dunes to the little oratory dedicated to St Piran, patron Saint of the Cornish. The wild flowers were an unexpected bonus, and the children had a great time trying to identify them. But I was filled with painful sadness at the pathetic appearance of the oratory, not far distant from the luxury holiday homes which dominate the footpath approach. Awful, blackened concrete roof protecting oratory, which is boarded up and inaccessible. We all felt a sense of shame that such a lovely setting should be spoiled by the very object which had drawn us there.'

It was said, although I did not know it at the time, that the good Saint was in the habit of decorating his Church with the choicest of flowers plucked, no doubt, from the rich variety which still bloom in such profusion around that once delightful and lonely oratory now decently and reverently buried out of the sight and reach of the latter-day Anglo-Saxons.

If, however, the oratory of St Piran has reaped a sterile harvest of sand, then a deep-seated fire in the summer of 1983 further along the coast, at Tintagel, gives rise to new hope about our understanding of Cornwall's Dark Ages. It is thanks to the Director of the Institute of Cornish Studies, Professor Charles Thomas, that the finds made on Tintagel Island after that fire, could link the 170 buildings which have

The oratory at Perranzabuloe was created in the sixth century. In 1910 it was covered with protective concrete to save it from three enemies – sand, water and vandals.

The Tintagel site was certainly used in the pre-Roman period.

been exposed – four times as many as indicated in the official guide book – with the lost Roman outpost of Durocornovium. A Roman connection is, however, purely conjectural at this stage.

However, the archaeologists have been able to establish that the Tintagel site was certainly in use in the post-Roman period. Discoveries of imported wheel-made pottery identifies a date of between AD 425 to 650 – i.e. the Age of the Saints. The report of the extraordinary and impressive range of imports leads its authors to infer that trade must have been conducted from the island with a customer or customers of some status. The rectangular shape of the buildings exposed by the fire has led the archaeologists to believe that they date from the twelfth or thirteenth centuries, contemporary with

24

the large, three-ward Tintagel Castle, so deep-rooted in the Arthurian saga, despite that fact that six or seven centuries separate the construction of the castle from the life and times of the 'Once and Future King.'

This was a kind of propaganda castle in any case. Writing about it in the annual review of the Royal Commission on Historical Monuments, Charles Thomas and Peter Thomas stated: 'The Earls of Cornwall perhaps fastened on Tintagel somewhat as Napoleon or Hitler might have cast eyes upon Windsor or the Tower of London. Tintagel, or Dyndagll, the fortress of the constriction – the neck of land to the island – was where the legendary kings of Cornwall had lived, where Tristan had brought back Iseult for King Mark, and where place, antiquity and tradition met to validate rule over the Cornish.'

What is most significant, however, for the future – as well as for the past, as I wrote in *The Western Morning News* at that time, (1985) – is that the relics now seen to be prodding above the earth and littering this Duchy of Cornwall-owned Tintagel Island, overlie the remains of a fifth to seventh century 'Seat of Status' and, perhaps, a Roman centre also.

Strenuous efforts have been made to investigate further the Tintagel story. Charles Thomas and Peter Thomas have warned that it will be the fault, communally, of a great many of us if the opportunity to investigate is shelved. On the grounds of scholarship, public education, public interest and, perhaps, even on those of commercial probity, the opportunity cannot be dismissed.

Is it possible that, during Cornwall's Age of the Saints, Tintagel was the seat of King Geraint, the Dingerein referred to in the life story of St Teilo? Remote, of course, it always has been, but we are well aware of the strong desire in the Celtic Church to withdraw from the seething world into wild and distant places. In that, it resembled more the Theban monks of Egypt, as archaeologist Aileen Fox says, who preferred to operate deep in the desert. They had perfectly good precedents for this behaviour, as the lives of Saint Paul and the fourth-century St Antony indicate.

Lady Fox argues that the monastery at Tintagel was founded in the sixth century by St Julian or Juliot, a child of King Brychan, with cells for around 30 monks. Their life would have been harsh and poverty-stricken in this wild setting. Yet, it seems, they were able to obtain wine and oil, required for their Services, from foreign

25

merchants, and food to sustain their basic needs. They also possessed, it appears, a sweat house – a sauna – from the evidence of a burnt, paved floor. Water was thrown on heated stones to provide them with a vapour bath in their eyrie perched some 250 feet up precipitous cliffs overhanging the shining Atlantic.

The vapour bath at Tintagel, along with the kiln for drying the corn, lends an air of unexpected luxury to the monastery at Tintagel. But the sweat house could have been the means of the occasional source of bodily discipline to these uncompromising Celts, and the corn would have been harvested only by the most careful and diligent husbandry from such a rocky, barren promontory.

In the endeavours to penetrate the veil of the Dark Ages, and to peer a little more closely into the life-style of these Saints, we have to rely upon archaeological assistance. The shadow of the Dark Ages was cast slowly over Europe as the Roman Empire, and the centuries of ordered peace which it brought, sank into decline after 410. Britain had been largely populated by the Celts. By men and women who were proud of their lineage as well as their smattering of the Latin tongue. The Nordic invasion had put paid to the hopes of a secure future, and many of those not butchered by the Anglo-Saxons fled westwards, away from the lowlands swept clean of Celts by the new broom from the north and the east of Europe.

The Saxons, having conquered, began to populate the empty lowland territories, and to evolve a civilisation which soon became superior to that of the so-called barbarous Celts skulking in the upland and mountainous regions of western Britain, and scratching out a living on poorer soil. It was centuries before the Saxons finally troubled to subjugate the wild men of the west. Not until the ninth or even the tenth century was their take-over complete, by which time even the Welsh were becoming accustomed to their neighbours.

Long before the process was complete, both sides were Christian. It was not the Celtic Saints, however, who were responsible for the conversion of the Anglo-Saxons. Their hatred of the heathen invaders who had committed wholesale massacre was such that they desired no contact at all. Their flock was to be found in the west. In Ireland and Wales, Strathclyde, in Devon and Cornwall, and in Armorica. It was in these areas that the Celtic race and customs survived to a large extent.

To the Nordic invaders – and, make no mistake, their impact

Tintagel Church drawn by Felicity Young.

upon the future of Britain was greater, by far, in almost every sense even than that of the Normans in 1066 – the concept of Christianity was wholly foreign and alien. They worshipped Odin and Thor, a warrior religion, in which no-one needed to trouble about the future of their eternal souls.

Their religion was more a code of honour than a philosophical discussion. Cowardice, desertion, lies, dishonour – these were the principal crimes in the eyes of the Nordic race, worse, much worse, than the slaughter of their fellow men. They sacrificed horses and cattle and celebrated with feasting and drinking.

But theirs was not a religion of dread. They were taught not to fear death. The ideal was the fellowship of the hero with the gods in some twilight Valhalla. It was not the Celtic Saints who converted these violent and aggressive creatures to Christianity. England, their new land, was ringed by the encircling fire of Christ's message, and the Anglo-Saxon lay directly in the advancing path of the religious teaching of Columba and Aiden from the North, and Gregory and Augustine from Rome, not to overlook, of course, the contribution of St Patrick, a Romanized Briton, whose conversion of Ireland between 432 and 461 started Christianity on the track back to Northern England.

As for the Celts, their conversion may be said to have begun more

27

than a century before St Augustine came to England, and for that they are indebted to St German of Auxerre, in France. It is to St German, more than any other, argues Canon Doble, that we owe so much. He was the spiritual father of Celtic Christianity and, says Doble, through his disciple, St Patrick, St German is also the spiritual father of Christian Ireland.

German, whose very name, in Latin, means Brother, was born at Auxerre, south of Paris in 380. His family were noblemen and, we are told, he was much happier following the hounds than in attending church. It is said that the barking of his hounds and the hooves of his horse disturbed more than one congregation of worshippers. In 418, he was ordained, and a miraculous conversion occurred in his whole character. The priesthood meant sacrifice to him. He distributed his money among the poor and slept on a bed of ashes.

This Gallo-Roman was sent by his Bishop to Britain to eliminate the heresy of Pelagianism, a creed which had been spread by a British monk. Of all the great schisms which were to split the Church of Rome, this was among the earliest, and it originated from a British monk, Peliagus. Essentially, he would not accept that, at birth, we all inherited 'original sin'. St German's mission between 429 and 447 was highly successful, and he was to die, honoured by the Church on July 31, 448.

St German had a gift for conversion, and it is claimed that he was the source of inspiration for those Britons who crossed over to the half-heathen Armorica in the second half of the fifth century and made it Christian Brittany. This champion of orthodoxy, accumulated no fewer than 27 episcopal tributes at his shrine.

But if the Anglo-Saxons were not yet ready to receive the Redeemer, how does it come about that the Celts were prepared to accept the teachings of Jesus Christ almost without reservation? It was an age which had a huge appetite for wonders and miracles. The Celts were a people whose vanity made them unbearable in victory, and downcast and despondent in defeat. And it must be remembered, they had recently suffered a crushing series of defeats at the hands of the Anglo-Saxons. Christianity was in every sense a cooling balm to these people.

They were indeed ready for Jesus Christ. Seeing the Abbot and his monks in the holiness of the monastery; listening to the strange but

St German's Church today – the Saint had a gift for conversion.

metrical lilt of the Latin – such magic in the beauty of the prayers; the tasting of the Communion bread; the touch of the rosary beads; the scent of the incense as it shrouded the little oratory – the very mystery of the incarnation itself. As Frank Delaney so exquisitely describes it in his book, The Celts, 'Religious belief provided the oxygen to Celtic aspirations to immortality.'

And yet, as with the conversion of the Anglo-Saxons which was to follow, there is a curious interwoven mixture of beliefs, with past habits creeping into this universal new Christianity. From what is known of the Celts, and their pagan past, this is hardly surprising. They held fire festivals every five years, when they were apt to sacrifice the human animal along with other beasts of burden in colossal images of wickerwork or grass and wood.

The anthropologist, Sir James Frazer, explains that the custom lingered on into the nineteenth century on the continent of Europe, though without live sacrifices. In Paris, they last took place in 1743 'to the strains of Salve Regina'. In Brie, Isles de France, a wickerwork giant was burnt on Midsummer Eve. There are instances of a column of serpents going up in fire in the Pyrenees, and at Metz, cats were burned since 'cats represented the devil, and could never suffer enough.' This kind of paganism happened many years ago, and hopefully would never be repeated in modern times.

Among British Celts, the chief fire festivals of the year appear to have been those of Beltane (May Day) and at Samhain or Hallowe'en (the last day of October). May Day is celebrated, of course, with a public holiday – but that seems to have its origins more in the Labour movement than in Celtic ritual. But observe the old Cornish customs which still surround that day – or watch, at Hallowe'en, the glimmering and flickering last remnants, the almost instinctive folk memory of the once pagan Celts. Were these dread giant wickermen, with their human cargoes, once fired on the uplands of Devon and Cornwall, as propitiation to the God of the Harvest? The answer is probably not – but how are we ever to know?

'The Christian calendar,' observed Frank Delaney, 'reinforced the regularity of worship, with recognition of the practical relevance of the Celtic festivals.' The conversion of the Celts was satisfactorily achieved on all sides, since Christianity offered so much more than negative, sterile pagan beliefs. Yet superstition lingers on, even up to the present day, and who can see the wisps of paper and linen which drape the trees and bushes around Madron Well, near Penzance, without seriously wondering about instinctive beliefs and those which are imposed from without?

The 'power' of Madron Well ranges from reported miracles to the merry rustic divination of a May morning when 'Two pieces of straw about an inch long are crossed and transfixed by a pin. This, floated on the water elicits bubbles, the number of which, carefully counted, denotes the year before the happy (wedding) day.' Such magicking almost certainly pre-dates not just the Age of the Saints, but the Celts themselves.

That remarkable Cornishman, A. K. Hamilton Jenkin, has written extensively of the Cornishman's high regard for holy wells. Madron, he says, has always been considered at its most potent for children suffering from skin complaints – and is best on the first three Wednesdays in May. A. K. Hamilton Jenkin puts in a good word also for several other wells. St Breward, for instance, St Nun's Well at

Madron Well ranges from reported miracles to the 'merry rustic divination of a May morning.'

Jesus Well, St Minver.

Altarnun, Alsia Well in Buryan, St Minver and Menacuddle, the wells of St Keyne, St Martin, St Merryn and Gulval . . .

'Within the hearts of old people, fragments of old time lore are treasured even now with a secret, half-ashamed conviction – a conviction which is revealed only in moments of extraordinary crisis or when in the company of those who have really become at one with the people through long and sympathetic acquaintance . . . many rare flowers of the imagination, a magic casement opening up upon innumerable vistas.' When put like this, who, but those with hearts of stone, could possibly resist the temptation to try. Mr Jenkin understood the Celt in all of us.

What kind of Devon and Cornwall was it that those Saints found? There is a powerful impression from most of the history books that it was a land swathed in deep forests. Yet that would not have been altogether the case. It seems that, at the most attractive and fascinating period of the history of the Westernmost counties, inscrutibility covers the landscape. Here, we need to use our imagination, with some sobering scientific assistance.

In his brilliantly comprehensive work, *The History of the Countryside,* Oliver Rackham says that it is a fallacy to suppose that upon the recall of the Roman Legions in the fifth century, the South West reverted to woodland. The great Domesday survey of 1086 makes it clear, says Mr Rackham, that England was not well wooded even by twentieth-century standards, let alone those of eleventh-century Europe. I suspect that statement will come as a considerable shock to many people. Large areas of Cornwall – the Lizard, Penwith, Bodmin Moor, North West Cornwall recorded no woodland at all in the Domesday survey.

Of the 767 woods recorded in Devon, half were smaller that 17 acres in extent. There were no boundless woodlands. And, he argues, the Lizard peninsula has altered little in the last 1,000 years – the woodland was confined to the steep sheltered valleys of the Helford River. But there was woodland around Padstow – a very important centre for the Celtic Saints – and Bodmin.

Mr Rackham, who is acknowledged as an authority, reckons that there was about four per cent woodland cover in Devon and some three per cent in Cornwall in 1086. But he offers this thought, and his words have the ring of authenticity about them: 'Possibly the most pervasive change which someone returning from the Middle Ages would note in the countryside is the appearance of the tree trunks.'

At a major public inquiry, in 1971, into a proposal to construct a huge oil-fired power station at Millbrook, on the banks of the River Tamar, some revealing evidence was given by two experts on lichen. They, too, pointed out the superabundance of lichens which then existed on trees removed from the polluting atmosphere, the acid rain, of the city conurbation at Plymouth. On the deeply wooded banks of the River Walkham, for example, at Horrabridge, where bearded lichens still hung in great drifts from the tree trunks. The tree trunks of the Middle Ages were similar. Clusters of diverse and colourful lichens and deep green mosses lending to the countryside in general a distinctive, if subtle, colouring. Nowadays, the average tree trunk is covered with a thin layer of an undistinguished single grey-green variety.

The Celtic Saints would have come to a region which was then alive with colour on the trees of the Ancient Countryside, the thorn and blackthorn, apple and elder, willow and ash, alder and elm, hazel and holly, aspen and yew. How lovely, and, yet lonely, a countryside this Land of the Saints would have seemed. A landscape rinsed with bluebells, pink with campion, then purple with the foxglove. A breathtakingly beautiful coastline drenched in seaholme and samphire, with wild hyssop, sage and marjoram, bee-infested rosemary and honeysuckle. A land where squab pie was one of the delicacies, where a harvest of herring and pilchards could be obtained from the sea and juicy shellfish waited to be picked from the rocks, of barley bread or potatoes. All they lacked, it seemed, was the understanding to convert this potential plenty to its fullest, if not its best, advantage.

But as the native or the would-be invader alike peered through the hems of mist which so often steal across our still beautiful counties of Devon and Cornwall, would they have seen much as we see today? Or were there notable differences, human habitation and the engineering handiwork of man apart? For that information, we can hardly do better than turn to another splendid book of the 1980s, Professor Charles Thomas's *Exploration of a Drowned Landscape,* the archaeology and history of the Isles of Scilly.

The sea itself has been rising at the approximate rate of about nine inches in every century, hence, in the period 450 to 600 AD, the level of the high-water mark could have been as much as 12 feet lower in places than it is today – a very considerable distance. In those times, the Isles of Scilly were almost certainly a land mass, to which those now delightful offshore islands were physically connected. In the case of the Scilly Isles, it is well within the mind's compass to link, for example, the islands of Bryher and Tresco. I, doubtless along with

The Celtic Saints would have come to a region which was then alive with colour on the trees of the Ancient Landscape.

dozens of other visitors, walked between the two places over dry sand in the autumn of 1985. It was also possible to walk from Bryher to Samson in knee-high water at low tide in that same October. Though for how many years longer this will be possible remains to be seen.

It is through Professor Thomas's book that there is a vision of the Scillies in the Age of the Saints when, for example, the island of St Helens, which boasted a Saint and his monastery, was no mere islet upon Tresco's flank, but an integral part of the mainland proper. How much more difficult it is, however, to imagine that extra 12 feet of land when standing, for instance, at Padstow gazing across at the vast estuary of sand between it and Rock. Or at Hayle, when the Saints came marching in. It opens up the extraordinary vista of a time when the many small rocks which decorate the coastline of Devon and Cornwall were once unwashed by the waves. Of a time when a forest surrounded St Michael's Mount — as is evident from the roots of trees which have been seen at times of low tide between the Mount and ancient Marazion.

The Cornish scholar, Dr A. L. Rowse, once wrote, in a literary connection, but the words would seem just as appropriate to the topographical one which we are now considering: 'But there are other evidences that tell us something of what we fain would know, evidences more continuous, more loquacious, though no less complete . . . and with tantalising silences.' The Age of the Saints as much as the Land of the Saints, might appear to be very much a part of history's blank page. But without those Saints, it would be almost a total blank.

An ancient manuscript, compiled by an unknown scribe, long after the death of St Mewan, recorded similar thoughts on the seeming historical emptiness of those ages: 'When all the world was wrapped in the errors of the Gentiles (heathens), the Son of God became incarnate and died for our redemption. His church grew and filled the earth, in spite of the efforts of the evil one to destroy it by raising persecutions, in which many martyrs died. At last, peace dawned for the church and men glorious with the light of faith, following in the footsteps of Christ, went forth into all the world . . .'

These 'Lives' were written down up to 500 or 600 years after the Age of the Saints. It is, as we have seen, in the place names that they are best remembered. But the Saints were real and substantial figures in their own lifetime, and not mere figments of the imagination. What is more, they brought the message of Christianity to the hearts and minds of men and women living in the Westcountry, when the remainder of Britain was being over-run by heathens and pagans.

Although these Celtic Saints never took it upon themselves to evangelize the Anglo-Saxons, they did cover their own remote and extensive territory with astonishing thoroughness. They seemed never to have stood still in their quest to spread the word of Christ. St Columba, for example, was said to have established around 100 monasteries in his lifetime, most, if not all of which, would have been created only after extensive travelling around his vast Northern 'diocese'. Recording his life's work was to keep the scribes especially busy.

One 'life' was, however, written up comparatively shortly after the death of a Saint. That concerned St Samson whose story, it is said, was composed by a scribe who obtained his information from an 80-year-old monk, who had heard stories about the Saint from a cousin who had conversed with Samson's mother.

If this seems a somewhat remote source, then a glance at the vast space in time covering the first five books of The Bible, for example, lends an authentic air to the composition of Samson's life, if not to many of the other written lives of the Saints. Of course they were embellished by writers eager and anxious to pile on the miracle-making. It not only added a scintillating flavour to spirituality – which was, after all, the writers' business as churchmen – but it added all-important mystery to the zeal of those early Celtic missionaries. The results are far from boring!

We are told that St Brigid was particularly adept as a brewer, and that lepers clamoured for her ale. But St Brigid, who obviously had no wish to be remembered as the Saint of Brewers, simply told those who sought the fine ale that the only liquor which she had to dispense was her bathwater.

It is not difficult to envisage the interpretation an imaginative scribe, writing centuries later, and eager to invest the Saintly Abbess with an aura of immortality, would place upon that story. He wrote, quite simply, and with awesome sincerity, that St Brigid's bathwater was miraculously converted into ale! The Lives of the Saints are replete with many kinds of symbolism, which, in themselves, hark back to earlier centuries, and to Nature worship.

The serpents and dragons inhabiting the dark caves were symbols of evil, and must be slain. They relate to the monstrous and reptilious behaviour of people as much, if not more than to real creatures. But

37

SAINT · SAMPSON

BAPTIZING · A · HEATHEN

Given · by · Horace · Hylton
parish · and · Caroline · his

Will · B.A · Curate · of · this
wife · Easter · 1891 · Ps · 105 · 2

taken literally, they lend a fairy-tale atmosphere to many of the stories of the Celtic Saints.

A number of these Celtic Saints were women but there is a certain obscurity about their role in the Church. By the time the Lives of the Saints were written up, between the twelfth and fourteenth centuries, the generally diminished role of women had been determined. The obligation of celibacy among the monks had seen to that. It is, in so many ways, a sad reflection upon many male attitudes which have lingered on into modern times, and which threatens to be carried on for a long time into the future.

That this antipathy towards women existed, as far back as the sixth century, is evident in the attitude of certain Bishops who severely criticised the Britons in Armorica for celebrating Eucharist in the presence of a woman named Conhospitae – 'A name,' they declared, 'which one cannot hear or pronounce without shuddering!' Poor Conhospitae. She may well have been the wife of one of the monks. Not all the monks, as we have seen, were ordained priests. Conhospitae apart, whose name in itself may have been a joke, and the cause of such tittle-tattle, it seems possible that women may have played a more significant role in the life of the early Church than the later, and more inhibited writers, were prepared to give them credit. And nowhere is this better illustrated than through the lives of the children of King Brychan of Wales – 12 men and 12 women, all of whom became Saints, or Martyrs.

It is almost certainly as a result of the extraordinary activities of Brychan's children that the old saying, 'There are more Saints in Cornwall than in Heaven,' came about. In Cornwall, there are said to be over 170 ancient parishes out of 212 dedicated to Welsh Saints – many, the progeny of Brychan. In Devon, the total is nearer 50. The inspiration, however, originated not only from Brychan, but also from Llantwit Major, in South Wales, where, in the fifth century, St Iltyd had created a monastery which taught many of the notabilities among the Celtic saintly fraternity.

It was from Llantwit that St Samson (circa 480 to 565) came to

The fine stained glass window at Golant Church shows St Samson – or Sampson in this case – baptizing a heathen.

Cornwall, landing at Padstow, and meeting up with the residue of monks from a previous mission at St Kew – Docco – before travelling along what we now know as the Saints Way towards Fowey. St Samson, as we learn from that valuable, and probably factual account written not long after he died, journeyed in a wagon across the Cornish peninsula, taking with him sacred books and holy vessels. Needless to say, the account of the journey was embellished with some piquant descriptions of pagans dancing around stones in Trigg Major, and some horse racing.

The Celts were excellent horsemen and some writers have reflected that had they turned this mastery to greater advantage, and developed the art of fighting on horseback, they might easily have dealt with the Anglo-Saxon menace on their boundaries. St Samson passed on, through Fowey, to Dol, in Brittany, where he was to make his name. A contemporary from Llantwit, St Petroc, remained in Padstow, where he founded a great monastery, before moving on to Bodmin, where he settled on land given him by the local rulers in the mid-sixth century. One of those rulers may have been King Constantine who, it is believed, was lording it over Dumnonia – Devon and Cornwall – by around 540 AD.

Many, and varied, are the sons and daughters of King Brychan of Brecknock – now, possibly, Hereford – in Wales. And, as may be seen in the Profile of the Celtic Saints drawn up at the end of this book, the names of those two dozen children were imprinted indelibly upon the place names of both Devon and Cornwall. Their names, and deeds, have fired the imagination of many writers, up to the present time.

Well worth mentioning, at this stage, is St Keyne, who, it is said, wandered over the lawless countryside of the time free from any risk of assault or insult by the mere strength of her purity. Inevitably, she performed miracles wherever she walked, and is remembered in Keynsham, in Avon, in particular, where she turned 'serpents' to stone, thereby rivalling St Hilda of the Northern Isles.

The power of turning flesh to stone has its origins even further back in antiquity. It is reminiscent of Perseus who struck off the

St Keyne Church. The Saint was said to have wandered over the lawless countryside free from any risk of assault or insult by the mere strength of her purity.

terrifying snake-wreathed head of the Medusa with one stroke of a sickle. Contacts between the South West and the Mediterranean were, moreover, older even than those between Devon and Cornwall and the Roman Empire.

It is not difficult to envisage how traders from the Eastern Mediterranean would have swapped fables with the Celts, who, themselves steeped in the art of story-telling, would have eagerly passed on these tales of myth and fantasy all round the Celtic kingdoms of the West. Even in the period 450 to 650 AD those eastern contacts were still much in evidence. At Tintagel, for example, where pottery has been unearthed indicating a quite inexplicable import trade in high quality consumables from Byzantium.

But St Keyne has other mythical links. Not least, she is said to have visited St Michael's Mount and bestowed upon it a now famous stone chair, in the church tower. Whichever of a newly married pair, bride or 'groom, first sits in this chair after their wedding, she, or he, will dominate the marriage. The water of St Keyne's well is said to possess the same 'powers'. The Victorian poet-laureate, Robert Southey found inspiration in the legend of St Keyne and her Holy Well. Ridicule such superstitions as most people invariably do, it is still generally believed that St Michael's Mount possesses many 'magical' qualities.

I have been told, for example, on the very best of authority, that when Mrs Margaret Thatcher visited the Mount not long before the General Election of 1979, which was to bring her to power for a record period of time, she was invited to touch the highest rock on the island, 'and to make a wish'. While she may be regarded, with justification, as a woman of a severely pragmatic character, she enthusiastically took the opportunity to make the contact. It was also abundantly obvious to her hosts precisely what the Prime Minister To Be had wished for! And since it was St Keyne who, above all other Saints, appeared to foster the desire to give women equal opportunities with men, then Margaret Thatcher could scarcely have chosen a more ideal spot upon which to make a personal wish.

Inevitably, this book has concerned the Celtic Saints of Cornwall much more than those of Devon, and the reason for this is simply the presence, from a relatively early stage, of the Anglo-Saxons, at the boundary of the River Tamar. The sub-Roman epoch of independence continued to flower in Somerset and Devon until the Saxon King

St Michael's Mount possesses many 'magical' qualities.

Centwine pushed the awkward Celts 'as far as the sea' in the year 682. Another 150 years were to elapse before first King Egbert in 838 and then King Athelstan (924 to 939), were finally to subjugate the Cornish Celts and their Christian rulers although, by that time, the Anglo-Saxons themselves had been converted to the faith.

The Celts, as a result of considerable petty in-fighting and feuding, were ill-equipped to resist the West Saxons when they decided to mop up and populate those areas of the country which their ancestors of the fifth century had decided virtually to ignore. And, being Anglo-Saxons, it is not surprising that they would impose upon the churches the Universal, as opposed to the Celtic titles to which many of the earlier foundations may have been dedicated. Indeed, the lack of Celtic Saints' names in the eastern half of Dumnonia – that is the county of Devon – leads one to suppose that the Anglo-Saxons may, very deliberately and consciously, have suppressed the earlier names which were to flourish throughout Dumnonia's western stronghold of Cornwall.

Devon's great historian, Dr W G Hoskins, is properly circum-spect, in the absence of firm evidence, about the influence of the Celtic Saints upon the development of Christianity in Devon and, as we have already seen, warns of the 'quicksands' into which every explorer after the truth can so quickly tumble. No less a figure than Professor Charles Thomas, in Cornwall, has also warned that the pattern or distribution map of particular Saints, places which are invested almost automatically with their deeds and lives, may, in the hands of the over-enthusiastic and less-learned, only create confusion.

Nothing like the same amount of attention – be it of an over-enthusiastic or even a less-learned kind – has been paid to the Celtic Saints of Devon as has been the case in Cornwall. But what Dr Hoskins calls 'funerary monuments' do survive in some numbers in Devon, many in the remote Northern part of the county. They are, for instance, to be found on Exmoor – Dartmoor's splendid array of crosses are of a much later period – on Lundy, Sourton Down (between Tavistock and Okehampton) and, somewhat oddly, in the vicarage garden at Tavistock.

One of these stones was found near Buckland Monachorum by the Reverend Atkyns Bray, a vicar of Tavistock, and served, he noted, as a quoin to the blacksmith's shop adjoining the churchard. Bray feared the massive stone might end up, as another in the district had done, as a gate-post, and he had it transported the five miles back to his vicarage garden, to the perpetual joy of his wife, Anna, who faithfully recorded the full details. Bray, however delighted – as did his novelist wife – in mixing a little fact with fancy. He was also an inveterate carver of stones, as his handiwork on great Dartmoor boulders in the bed of the River Cowsic demonstrates to this day. But there is no doubting the authenticity of the Buckland stone.

There are, in Devon, no fewer than 18 dedications to the Welsh Saint, Petroc, who, as we have seen, made Padstow and finally Bodmin his base.

And is there a hint of King Brychan, father of all those Cornish Saints, in the dedication to St Brannoc, or Brynach, at Braunton? Is it possible, asks Dr Hoskins, that the remains of this Welsh missionary Saint lie buried somewhere beneath the high altar?

Landkey, a parish to the South East of Barnstaple, certainly appears to suggest a more than passing acquaintance with St Kea. It was close by, in the sixth century, says the historian, that a

In Devon there are no fewer than 18 dedications to the Welsh Saint Petroc who made his Cornish base at both Padstow and Bodmin.

monastery was founded in the warm and fertile valley. The Anglo-Saxons may have been successful in ensuring the dedication of the church to the Universal St Paul, but the memory of St Kea, who was said to have been a young Irish Saint, lives on in the name, Landkey.

As if to reinforce our suspicions, just four miles distant is Filleigh, where the church nowadays is also dedicated to St Paul. But we know, from the lives of the Celtic Saints, that St Kea and St Fili were boon companions, and their names crop up together in Cornwall, at St Kea and Philleigh! Kea's name is also linked with that of St Rumon, whose name is indelibly bound with the magnificent foundation of Tavistock Abbey, created in 974, and in which the Saint's relics are said to have rested until snatched away by the King's men at the time of the dissolution in 1539.

Tavistock Abbey was the greatest monastic foundation west of Glastonbury – and it is hardly surprising, in the circumstances, that both Kea and Rumon were said to have been trained at ancient Glastonbury before beginning their missionary work in Devon and Cornwall. But many of the old dedications have been forgotten, or, suggests Dr Hoskins, 'deliberately changed' into something now quite unrecognisable, such as St Winwalloe at Portlemouth, in the far south of the county, which was rededicated to St Onolaus.

The Celtic Saints were active in Devon. Of that there can be no doubt, and they founded a number of their tiny monasteries on the coasts and river banks, though nothing as majestically beautiful, of course, as the later foundation at Tavistock which, for all its dedication to St Rumon – and St Mary – was very much an Anglo-Saxon concept. Not, of course, that the Celts themselves completely ignored, or were opposed to, the dedication of a church or monastery to one of the more universal Saints – St Mary, St James, St Paul, St Peter, or other Apostles, for example.

There is even speculation that close ties existed between the Abbey of Glastonbury and that at Exeter where, in the seventh century, St Boniface was educated. The Exeter Monastery, or Abbey, was a Celtic foundation, and, it is said, a daughter establishment of the great Glastonbury. How can anyone do better than quote Dr Hoskins on the association between the Celtic Saints and Devon. 'In ancient sunlight, the Celtic Saints sailed up the tidal waters of the Taw, and walked on its shores through lorn autumns and triumphant Springs.'

Equally, as a man of West Devon, I like to think of the Celtic Saints, such as St Budoc and those friends, St Indract and St Dominic, sailing into the Plymouth Sound at the beginning of these Dark Ages. There is a Cathar-ish quality about these Celtic Saints. The Perfecti, a few centuries later, preached and travelled in pairs. Their preaching was considered heretical, however, and they were savagely crushed.

The wooded slopes of Mount Edgcumbe and of Devonport would have seemed so tempting to these travellers. Budoc chose the eastern bank, founding his monastery at Budshead – Budoc's Hide – not far from the tiny port of Tamerunta – Tamerton Foliot – now lost in a

The broad stretch of the River Tamar.

muddy creek. Indract and St Dominic selected the Cornish side of the Tamar to site their monasteries, long before the days the Edgcumbes emerged from Milton Abbot to create the grey fortress-like structure of Tudor Cotehele.

Indract and St Dominic would have come to know the area intimately, from the great sea bulwark of Rame Head, right up to ancient Callington and Kit Hill beyond. Budoc would have roamed across the forest wastes where the city of Plymouth now lies. He might have paused, from time to time, high above the modern city at the point we now call the Blockhouse, the site, perhaps, of an ancient hillfort in even earlier times. It would have afforded him a magnificent vista – as it does, to this very day – of the approaches to Plymouth, and the broad stretch of the River Tamar to the west. To the south loomed the Mount Batten headland, which is known to have been a pre-Roman point of tin trading contact. Budoc went on to Rome, and to fame in the early Chruch.

A thousand or more years were yet to elapse before Drake, Hawkyns and the restless Elizabethans, were to make this a port to be reckoned with, before the little Mayflower plunged past these headlands to found a mighty new nation far across the shining shield of the Atlantic.

This great port was then but a quiet backwater, where salmon flirted with the shadows cast by great trees on the riverbank. A rivermouth unpolluted by the teeming activities of mankind, a shore-line untainted and untouched by dockyards and nuclear activity, leading to a valley whose huge wealth in minerals lay only a few feet beneath the surface – the glittering prize of a copper kingdom. Theirs for the taking. Indract, Budoc and Dominic had their minds set, however, on an even mightier harvest than salmon or copper. They sought the immortal souls of men. As Dr Hoskins puts it: 'Walking beside these estuaries and over these headlands, one treads on holy ground, where the Celtic Saints once walked in the freshness of the early world.'

Little, if anything of substance, remains in the way of evidence where once they walked. A collection of crosses, comparatively abundant in number in Cornwall, but thinning and petering out as they reach the eastern boundaries of North Devon. Ogham lettering, like Morse code, engraved upon their granite surfaces, and messages in Latin, proclaiming some as grave-stones. As time went on, and shadowy memories of Rome receded, the spelling fumbled and faded.

The many Celtic crosses which still abound in Cornwall.

Many of the great stones survived, however. Few of the small circular stone dwellings did. Some of the old hill forts, created long before the Romans came, were re-occupied. The practical Normans, with their love of castles, were yet to arrive upon the scene.

One of the clues to the life-style of these Celtic people is to be found in the pottery which they used. Jars and plates, mixing bowls of good quality, have been found at Porthmeor, Tintagel and on the Isles of Scilly. These examples are known as Gwithian-style. But towards the end of the fifth century, a striking change occurred, which appears to coincide with the influx of the Irish between 450 and 500 into the River Camel area, around Padstow.

Coincidentally, a new type of pottery began to emerge, redder in appearance than the old due to a difference in manufacture. And the undersides of that new pottery provides the archaeologists with a vital clue as to its probable origins. For it bore the impression of chopped, dried grass, obviously employed to prevent the clay from sticking to the slab on which it stood for baking. The grass-marked pottery is, however, to be found in one other place in Europe only at that time, the North East corner of Ireland. It provides an important clue between the movement and contact of the peoples of that era.

Yet to be explained, however, is the presence at Tintagel Island of large quantities of pottery ware from such exotic climes as Egypt and Byzantium as well as from France and the Rhineland. Astonishingly, these little shards of clay are sure pointers to the past, more telling and revealing than skeletons of fragile man or the huge stone monuments which he set up over the dead.

But the twilight of the Celtic Saints was closing in as the pressures, both physical and spiritual, from the east began to build up relentlessly. The evangelization of the Anglo-Saxon invaders began in the South East of England with the arrival of St Augustine in 597. In the North, St Oswald, St Paulinus and the Irish St Aiden were active. Augustine was the emissary of Gregory who, it is said, had seen in the Roman slave-market a group of blue-eyed, fair-haired Anglo-Saxon youths. He made inquiries about them and their country. Convert these Angles to Angels was the papal instruction issued to Augustine. Bishop Augustine needed further encouragement before he and his fellow missionaries returned to England after their initial failure among the Angles. Small wonder the Christian Celts would have nothing to do with converting such heathens.

But Augustine was rejected also by the Celtic clergy at a meeting near the mouth of the River Severn some years later. The parties quarrelled, and one can imagine how Augustine fumed over these extraordinary wild-looking Celts with their long hair and severe tonsures, which may have reminded him more of the descriptions given by the ancient Romans of Druid priests than of Christian Saints. Augustine withdrew to Kent where he was to found the See of Canterbury. Pagan London, where he had hoped to create a great Christian centre, had flung out the missionaries from its midst. But there were signs that the barriers between Celt and Saxon were crumbling. Indeed, to such a degree that the Christian Welsh, under King Cadwallon, united with the Woden worshipper, Penda of Mercia, to inflict savage revenge upon Northumbria.

However, the differences between the Celtic and the Roman churches, identified, but not settled at their quarrelsome Severn-side conference, began to take on troublesome new dimensions as, from

Iona and the North, the Celtic Saints begain to infiltrate Saxon soil. As long as they were out of sight in their Western strongholds, they were also out of mind, it would seem.

The Roman church seized on the differences between the Christian cults. Even on the manner in which the Celts cut their hair. The Roman priests cut round tonsures on their crowns. They made an issue out of haircuts! Trivial as that may now seem to us, it was the surface friction of far more fundamental issues of spirit and of organisation. Underlying such petty squabbles was the whole question of submission not, as might be thought, to the will of Christ, but to the will of Rome.

The brothers in God met again at the Synod of Whitby in 664 and the Celts were outflanked by Oswy, King of Northumbria, who gave judgement in favour of Rome as the inheritors of Peter's commission. Some of the Saints, like St Cuthbert, drifted back into the great wilderness. Others were bewildered as to their future role, but Whitby marked a turning point. The Celts had been outwitted and, over the coming centuries, Scotland and Wales, Ireland and Devon and Cornwall fell in line with the rest of Europe.

There can be little doubt, however, that the Council of Whitby was where the seeds of trouble for the Roman Church were sown. It formed part of the bitter whirlwind of a harvest, reaped hundreds of years later, when the Reformation swept across Europe. It is not difficult to understand the meek acceptance by the majority of Celts of Oswy's settlement. It held out a promise of a new Springtime for Europe – of a return to the ordered existence when the Romans were in charge. There may have been many doubts and suspicions, but few regrets among the Celts, who had been at war with their neighbours, and among themselves, for almost 250 years. Unity was the way forward. Sadly, as the unfolding centuries ahead were to reveal, that unity of purpose foundered in fallible hands – man's not God's.

As with all things, the new order took time to filtrate into the remote regions of Cornwall and Devon. And it mattered not an iota to the fresh pagan force from the North, the Viking warriors. They broke over this nascent nation like the wrath of the Almighty. From fiord and sand-dune, Norway and Denmark, they launched themselves upon the Empire of Charlemagne, and the England of Alfred. Devon and Cornwall suffered from their attacks. The little coastal monasteries were easy targets for their pillaging activities until the sea-raiders themselves finally succumbed to the Christian message.

But there is more than a hint that the Cornish Celts were even more reluctant than their neighbours to abandon old and established ways. The Council of Whitby's decisions appeared to have passed over their heads. After the golden age of the Saints, information about the activities of the Cornish Church diminished. Clearly, the Anglo-Saxons felt that no exception could be made to the Universal Church. But it was not until the year 838, almost two whole centuries after the Whitby Synod, that the Saxons, under King Egbert, defeated a combined Cornish and Viking force at the battle of Hingston Down near Callington.

Even the temporary alliance with the Danish raiders could no longer stem the process, begun by Centwine in 682, of opening up the old Celtic areas to prying foreigners. In the ninth century, Cornwall finally 'bent its neck' to the See of Canterbury when, it is said, the Cornish Bishop, Kenstec of Dinurrin (Bodmin) professed his obedience, and that of the remnants of the Celtic Church, to

The ruins of the old priory at Bodmin. And it was from Bodmin, or Dinurrin, that the Cornish Bishop Kenstec professed his obedience to Ceolnoth the Archbishop of Canterbury.

St Germans became the Christian centre of Cornwall.

Ceolnoth, the Archbishop of Canterbury.

That the Cornish themselves were not entirely content with the new arrangement can be gauged from the fact that, having created the See of Crediton early in the tenth century, King Edward invited its Bishop, Eadwulf, to stamp on any Cornish resistance to papal decrees. Under King Athelstan, St Germans became the Christian centre of Cornwall. The Church of Rome had finally triumphed, and the three great centres of Celtic worship, at Pawton – St Petroc – Gerrans and St Germans were almost wholly claimed by the Bishop of Crediton, who was an occasional visitor to these far-flung outposts from the year 909 onwards. The process was finalised in 1050, with the foundation of the See of Exeter, to which the whole of Cornwall became subservient.

Still wrapped in the mystique of their Celtic Saints and in the aura of Arthur's epic courage, the Cornish remembered with affection and reverence such endurance and self-denial. The little Kingdom was a remote, and often distant and detached country, with its own ways and its own beliefs. The unworldliness of the Saints had deeply affected their rich Celtic imagination and long memories. The Celtic memory is a strength and a weakness. A blessing – and a curse. On the moors, by the wayside and in the cemeteries, they were constantly reminded, by the 400 or so great Celtic crosses – the inscribed stones – of what once had been.

Nicholas Roscarrock, the Catholic Cornishman suffering confinement in Lord William Howard's home at Naworth, wrote with affection of his own county and its Celtic heritage: 'But there are things more intangible than this – the memories and myths that haunt the mind of a people. No peoples are so haunted by memory as the Celts, therein lies their distinctiveness in Europe.'

Now, perhaps, the Saints themselves are merely a part of folklore, and quite forgotten in their role of great ascetic missionaries who led our ancestors out of the terrifying nightmare world of vengeful spirits abiding in dark places, to the light of Christ's teachings. They were indeed, Heralds of Light. They brought to Cornwall, and to Devon, the radiant message of hope 'when all the world was wrapped in darkness'. Theirs was the robust and wholesome simplicity of a truly 'catholic' religion. They created a living church alive with buoyant, brave and colourful personalities. A church, untouched and untroubled by the great chasms of thought into which the bigots of later times were to cast it.

Prejudice dictates that we continue to call the period in which they lived and worked The Dark Ages. Yet how much darker was the world at their demise. We may read that after the dread Millennium passed – the year 1,000 AD with all its dire prognostications about the end of the world – that men breathed easier. 'It was as if,' wrote the monk Radulphus Glaber, 'the world was shaking itself to cast off its old age and was clothing itself everywhere in a white robe of churches.'

How astonished those early Christian Fathers would have been to see where their work would have carried the great faith. It was all part of the process which we in modern times continue. We have to contend with political and religious differences which that band of Celtic Saints could never have begun to fathom. Yet, in their own epoch, the great thirsty deserts far to the south had begun to embrace Islam. The boundaries had begun to close in.

The historic reminders of the Lives of the Saints are few enough, piled one on top of the other. Yet, mercifully, reminders there are still. In a place name, a figure of speech and, over the memorable landscape of Dumnonia, changed as it is. The legends live on. Not, perhaps, with the virility or the purity to be found beneath a Greek sky, but the echoes from the ancient past in Devon and Cornwall are there for those with a desire to listen. To walk along the footpaths trodden by these Celtic Saints serves to enhance, even uplift, the variety and quality of our own lives. To read about them, or to make a study of their achievements, inspires a sense of the wondrous freshness of a world of simple, but dramatic contrasts. Of a time when innocence and wickedness could be defined with the childlike clarity of a fairy story.

Yet our Saints, for they are ours in the same sense in which the Christ's Apostles made their mark initially upon the Mediterranean countries, are virtually ignored and forgotten. They, too, were true Apostles of Christ, though their fame was confined to the cold and remote north-western edge of Europe, far from Rome, and appreciated only as an outpost of Christianity. With crusading zeal, these Saints brought to lives that were brutish and brief the love of Christ. How could we ever forget them?

Notable Saints

ST AUSTOL AND ST MEWAN

St Austell is now a bustling, lively Cornish town, the capital of the county's clay industry, with its world-wide contracts and contacts. Its patron Saint was a hermit, and his friendship, with his kinsman, St Mewan, who was said to have been born in Gwent, and related to St Samson, is one of the gentlest and most touching pieces of sentiment in all hagiography. The parishes adjoin each other.

Leland recorded that 'St Austol and St Muen were greate friends whose parishes joyne and enjoye some priviledges together and they lived here together.' According to the Elizabethan writer, Nicholas Roscarrock, St Mewan's feast day is November 19. The later Cornish hagiographer, Canon Doble, accused the local historian, Canon Hammond, of trying to make a mystery of it! According to the Vita, written in the eleventh century, almost 500 years after the death of these two Saints, St Austol who was wont to serve his Godfather, St Mewan, humbly, wept exceeding when, in June, 627, he realised that he was dying. 'Who shall guard thy feeble sheep from the wolf when the shepherd is taken away?' sobbed Austol. 'By God's mercy,' the dying Saint replied, 'after seven days have elapsed, thou shall join me in the glory of heavenly life. The bond of charity which unites us is not broken, nay, it shall be made stronger.'

St Mewan died on June 21. Seven days later the monks found the body of Austol, who had undertaken a three day fast, lying dead in

St Austol was a hermit but had a gift of great friendship.

56

peaceful repose. When they visited the tomb of St Mewan they were astonished to discover that: 'The Saint's body, which diffused a fragrant odour, had moved, and was lying on the right of the grave facing the vacant space on the left, as if waiting for his disciple.' And thus, wrote the author of the Life of St Austol and St Mewan, the dead bones of the two Saints declared the love which had ever united them, and the power of that charity which covereth a multitude of sins ('And above all things have fervent charity among yourselves: for charity shall cover the multitude of sins.' I Peter 4.8).

The joint cult of these two Saints exists in Brittany, as well as in Cornwall, and is an excellent example of the 'pairing' of Saints, seen elsewhere between Cadoc and Mawgan, Kea and Fili, David and Nonna. It pre-dates the Cathar experience by several centuries, in which the Perfecti were accustomed to travel and to preach in pairs. But the close friendships which developed was one of the factors which the opponents of Catharism cited as an example of its wickedness. It was savagely stamped out in France in the thirteenth century, but has re-emerged from time to time, not least in our own twentieth century.

St Austell church at the heart of a bustling, lively Cornish town.

ST BONIFACE

He was believed to have been born in Crediton; the twelfth centenary of his death was observed in Devon in 1954. Although Boniface was not a Celtic Saint, his history is bound up with the events of the time and he was, in many respects, the greatest man of religion ever produced in Devon. Born Winfrith, in or about the year 680, St Boniface first studied at the Benedictine establishment in Exeter, the ruins of whose walls may still lie buried to this day beneath the Cathedral.

After training at Exeter, which is said to have enjoyed close links with Glastonbury Abbey, Winfrith moved to Nursling, in the diocese of Winchester, when he was 14, to a monastery of which he was to become the Abbot, but which was destroyed by Danish raiders in the ninth century. Winfrith met Archbishop Britwald at Canterbury, and visited Rome on many occasions. In 716 he travelled to Friesland and, after a further visit to Rome, where the saintly Pope Gregory II created him Bishop, he became the first preacher of Christianity in central Germany.

It is in Germany where he is most highly regarded, his fame being on a par with that of St Patrick in Ireland. Pope Gregory III appointed him an Archbishop by sending him the pallium, or cloak of office. Boniface, as he was now known, founded the famous monastery of Fulda in Bavaria in 741. His achievements in Germany compare with those of St Augustine in England, and it was he who was invited to crown Pepin, father of Charlemagne, at Soissons.

Boniface drew on the English monasteries for his preachers, and many left this country – monks and nuns – to place themselves in his service. He was a fervent missionary, much in the manner of the Celtic Saints, and he was martyred for his crusading zeal. It was upon the bank of the River Borne in Friesland, where he was murdered, along with a group of followers, including St Eoban, whom he had entreated not to arm themselves. 'Let us not fear those who may kill the body but cannot touch the soul,' he said, and died, as he had lived, without flinching. His feast day is celebrated on June 5. Boniface's body was taken to Fulda, where it remains to this day.

ST ELIDIUS

What connection is there between an imposing Victorian square in one of Devon's loveliest inland towns, Tavistock, and a tiny chapel on a deserted island on the Isles of Scilly? The answer is Saint Elidius, whose final resting place is almost certainly the delightful, but remote and uninhabited St Helen's, and to whose memory a shrine might have been created by monks of the Benedictine glory that was Tavistock Abbey. Nowadays, what remains of the Abbey, stripped as it was by the Henrican vandals in July, 1539, lies buried beneath the soil in the old cemetery of the Tavistock Parish Church, fronting the town's Victorian Bedford Square.

But what has St Elidius to do with Tavistock Abbey? It is simply that King Henry I gave the Isles of Scilly to the Abbey in 1114, and the monks of Tavistock would scarcely have wasted any opportunity to advertise that their possessions now included the saint-endowed Scillies. The fact that their colony was even more liberally pirate-endowed appeared not to matter. Unlike his namesake, Henry I did his best to safeguard and promote Tavistock, which established a priory on Tresco, not far from St Helen's. Many centuries earlier, the islands were linked by dry land before the rising sea fragmented the mainland (see *Exploration of a Drowned Landscape by Charles Thomas published by Batsford in 1985*). Among the early Celtic Saints associated, by name, with the Isles of Scilly are Samson, Awana, Theona, Elidius and Maudetus. St Mary, Martin and Nicholas are Universal Saints.

Maudetus, an Irish Prince, may have travelled to the north coast of Brittany via the Scillies. He is remembered there through the name, Isle Modez, near the delightful French port and yachting marina of Paimpol. During the 1950s, a church was excavated on St Helen's, showing it to have been 26 feet by 14. Beneath the floor of the aisle was a rock-cut grave, a cist within a fissure in the granite. This, it is thought, could have been the final resting place of St Elidius. Also discovered was part of a Purbeck marble shrine with a stone container which might well have contained the exhumed and disarticulated skeleton of the Founder himself. The patron Saint of St Helen's (St Elidius) was male. We know little else about him except that when William of Worcester copied details from the Kalendar at Tavistock Abbey he noted that Elidius – 'whose body lies in the island of Scilly' – was a bishop and confessor whose feast day is celebrated on August 8. The marble shrine found in the excavation on St Helen's might have been created especially at Tavistock Abbey.

ST KEVERNE AND ST JUST

The north-eastern half of the Lizard Peninsula, comprising Mawgan, St Martin, Manaccan, St Anthony and St Keverne, is popularly referred to as Meneage. That, in turn, is thought to be connected with manach, a monk, and implies monkish land. So thought the Cornish scholar, Charles Henderson, who concluded that there was, probably, a number of small monasteries in that area. Nowadays the locality is known through the great house of the Vyvyan family, at Trelowarren.

In considering the Celtic St Keverne and his life, we again come to this 'pairing', as we saw with St Austol and St Mewan. St Kevene's

Parish Church, St Just.

St Just Church on an Edwardian picture postcard. The Saint himself pledged his devoted brotherhood to Saint Keverne.

61

particular friend was his neighbour, St Just, and the principal tale concerning this pair reads almost like an Aesop Fable. Again and again, we are told, St Just pledged his devoted brotherhood to St Keverne. Heaven, it is said, was to witness the purity of their friendship 'and to the world they were to become patterns of ecclesiastical love.' But St Just envied St Keverne the possession of a particularly beautiful cup from which the brother was apt to drink long and deep of excellent wine.

One day, after a visit from his neighbour, St Keverne discovered that the drinking vessel was missing. Had temptation proved too great even for the saintly Just? Keverne, deeply angry, set out in hot pursuit of his friend, picking up and pocketing a few stone 'pebbles' at Crowza Down. St Keverne caught up with the retreating figure of St Just at Tre-men-keverne, and raced up the hill towards him. He called on St Just to stop – but that made no impression at all. Taking a stone from his pocket, he hurled it after St Just. That seemed to have the desired effect. St Just, realising that the game was up, untied the chalice, which was fastened to his girdle, and let it fall to the ground. Then, without so much as a backward glance, he ran as fast as his legs would carry him. St Keverne, puffing and panting, and out of breath, finally caught up and recovered the fallen chalice. There was little point in further pursuit, so Keverne hurled the Crowza stones at the retreating Just.

Those stones, each weighing hundreds of pounds, are there to this day. Efforts to remove them are said to be in vain. They may be carried away easily enough during the day, but return to their original positions by night! Presumably, Keverne and Just settled their differences with brotherly libations of wine.

ST LUDGVAN

Many cool Cornish streams flow into wells, and around these have built up a series of romantic legends, a number of which are inevitably linked with the Celtic Saints. One such story concerns St Ludgvan whose prayer for water was answered by the appearance of a crystal clear stream. The Saint washed his eyes in the sparkling liquid, and, dramatically, discovered that it enabled him to see microscopic objects. After more prayer, he drank the water, and found that he now possessed great fluency of speech. Again he prayed, that all children baptized in this stream should be spared the hangman's cord.

The power of this water to confer such a blessing was soon put to the test. During one baptism, the infant in Ludgvan's arms called on the name of the Satan, and the Saint was obliged to perform an exorcism. The Devil is said to have appeared before the terrified people, growing to a gigantic size, before spitting into the well water and ruining its power to give microscopic sight and the gift of great oratory.

The Devil, however, had overlooked the water's magical virtue of ensuring that any child in which it was baptized would be safe from being hanged by a silken cord. Satan, despatched to the Red Sea by Saint Ludgvan, vanished in a great flash of lightning, which brought down one of the pinnacles of the church. As it happens, changes in the law appear to have made the power of Ludgvan's well redundant, though it is said that no child baptized in its cool and crystal waters ever needed fear the hangman's noose.

ST NEOT

Though diminutive in height, St Neot possessed the will of a giant. In these days of the conservationist creed, Small is Beautiful, St Neot must rank high on any list of patron Saints of the environment. It is said that he was so small that when he celebrated Mass, he was obliged to stand on an iron stool at the altar. The stool, claimed Baring-Gould, was preserved at Glastonbury.

The church at St Neot provides a constant and beautiful reminder of the Saint's life. The stained glass windows are irreplaceable and can be counted among the most glorious of all Cornwall's treasures.

Not far distant from the present church, built long after little Neot had joined the company of Saints, is a holy well, in whose chilly waters he was accustomed to immerse himself. He was there one day chanting his psalms when a frightened, trembling doe appeared, hotly pursued by hounds. The creature pleaded with its eyes, and Neot dealt with the hounds. They fled from his stony glare. So impressed was the huntsman by what he had witnessed, that he abandoned the chase and presented Neot with his hunting horn.

Neot's love of wild creatures, especially the timid deer, is also borne out by a story of how, when the monastery's oxen were stolen, he harnessed the wild creatures to the plough at seed-time. Thereafter, the deer bore a white ring around their necks, and were safe forever from the hunt.

On yet another occasion, Neot, who had been given three fishes for his well, fell ill. The fishes, he was told, would last his lifetime as long as he daily took only one at a time for food. His servant, unaware of the agreement, and eager to please Neot, took two fishes from the well. One he boiled, the other he baked. But the Saint was distraught, and prayed long and hard over the dead fish. He ordered his servant to return the fish to the well and, as soon as they touched the water, they swam away with the third fish, unharmed. These miraculous stories, very much part of Cornish folk-lore, have been re-told, for ages past, to countless numbers of visitors through the medium of the stained glass in St Neot church.

St Neot Well in whose chilly waters the Saint immersed himself.

Hartland, the formidable Devon headland, is the centre of the cult of St Nectan, but the Saint, the eldest of King Brychan of Brecknock's very large family, has strong Cornish connections also. St Nectan was acknowledged by his brothers and sisters as their leader, and his fame spread far and wide beyond Devon and Cornwall, where there are five dedications to him, into Brittany where two places, between Quimper and Pont l'Abbe, are named after him – Lan-neizant and Kerneizan. Nectan belongs to the class of Saint who, in the language of the hagiographer, are called 'cephalophores'. Quite simply, it means that after being decapitated such Saints are said to have carried their heads in their hands!

There are numerous examples. It was in the remote area of North Devon that an important Abbey of Augustinian Canons, founded in 1169 by Jeffrey de Dinham, acknowledged Nectan as its patron. Nearby Welcombe also claims the Saint as its patron. In the twelfth century, William de Botrell gave the church at Forrabury to Hartland Abbey. Not far from Forrabury in the Tintagel direction is a deep and enchanting valley which opens to the sea near Bossiney Haven. At the head of this valley is a splendid cascade of water, some 40 to 50 feet in height. The rock over which the water tumbles has two basins, the lower of which is known as St Nighton's Kieve – a keeve being the word for a large tub or vessel used in brewing.

The writer, Wilkie Collins, gave up in despair at ever seeing this kieve, the 'nymph of the waterfall' at that time being a greedy farmer who demanded a fee before any visitor was allowed on the land. St Nectan's silver bell was said to have been thrown into the kieve after his death, where it buried itself in the river bed. It has given rise to many legends of wealth beneath the water.

St Nectan – or Nighton – was also honoured through chapels, one near St Winnow, another at Ashcombe in South Devon, another in the parish of Chulmleigh, in Devon, or so Canon Doble informs us, through a chapel-at-ease called St Nighton's east of Lostwithiel on the edge of Boconnoc Park, and yet another at Newlyn, about five miles south of Newquay, which once stood in the north-west corner of a field called Pepper Ground close to the point where the Newquay road meets the Newlyn to Cubert road. St Nectan, as the fist-born of King Brychan, was clearly a figure to be reckoned with from Hartland

St Nectan's Glen in North Cornwall with its famous waterfall near Tintagel.

to Padstow and beyond.

It is to William of Worcester that we must turn for the scraps of information about the Saint's life – and it is all too brief. In just two sentences, copied, perhaps, from a fuller account of Nectan's life, which William may have read in the Kalendar at Launceston, we learn a little of the local Hartland legends – of the church, and the holy well, and a particular rock nearby with a red streak in it. Then, without further ado, of Nectan's death 'by these robbers'. The murdered Nectan, it seems, carried his severed head to a well, and stepped from mortality to martyrdom.

ST RUMON

This Saint was known as Moronoc in Ireland, and was a member of St Senen's group, which came across to Cornwall at the end of the fifth century. Three Cornish churches carry his founding name, as well as a chapel at Polruan, opposite Fowey. Local pronunciation and variations in spelling, a besetting problem for all engaged in a study of the Celtic Saints, has resulted in this Saint's name emerging in many varieties. As Lantaran, Lanruan, Ruan, Roman and, to complete the tangle, his name is often confused with the Breton Saint Ronan.

But it is evident that St Rumon was buried at Ruan Lanihorne, where his tomb was held in the deepest veneration. Around the year 980, Ordulf, brother-in-law of King Ethelred, and founder of the great Tavistock Abbey, commanded that the Saint's remains should grace the new Abbey church. Since no-one dared refuse the King's high-reeve (the Queen, Elfrida, was his sister), the relics were transferred over the Tamar into Devon. It is possible that the Vita, or account of the Saint's life, which invariably accompanied a Saint's relics, was also brought to Tavistock, and may have been destroyed when the first Abbey was burnt by the Danes when they attacked it in 997.

But the itinerant writer, Leland, claimed to have seen a copy of the life of St Rumon in the Tavistock Abbey library centuries later. That, it is now believed, was simply an adaptation of the biography of the Breton St Ronan. It seems that Rumon, although coming to Cornwall from Ireland, where he had been born, was probably trained at Glastonbury. The three Cornish churches which bear his name are at Ruan Lanihorne, on the Fal, and Ruan Major and Ruan Minor on the

St Rumon, on the left, in the stained glass window at Tavistock Church.

Lizard. In North Devon, he is patron of Romansleigh.

It seems probable that Rumon was a member of that exalted band of martyred cephalophores, since it was a headless body which rested in Tavistock. In the fourteenth century, the Abbey of Glastonbury was said to have secured one of the Saint's bones among its prized relics. But it was an era when forgeries were rife, and the glories of Glastonbury and Tavistock were transient. In March, 1539, the Abbot of Tavistock and his 20 monks assembled in the curiously hewn and carved stone octagonal chapter house, taking their place for the last time in their accustomed stalls. They signed the deed of surrender to King Henry VIII and the sycophant Cromwell. The gold, silver and jewelled ornaments which lay at the shrine of the Celtic Saint Rumon were carted away – to Henry's treasure house, in the Tower of London. The churchwardens paid the 'kings visitors' who cleared away stones and bones from the churchyard – St Rumon's, doubtless, among them – a fee of precisely two pence.

If Boniface is the most famous Saint among Germans, and Patrick the Irish, then it is St Samson for the Bretons. He is also the patron Saint of little Golant, on the Fowey River, and of South Hill. Samson was a Welsh bishop, and chief among the seven great Saints of Brittany, and, as we have already noted, his life story is the earliest and therefore probably the most authentic of any of his contemporaries in Wales, Brittany or Cornwall.

At the tender age of five years, he was taken to the monastery of Llantwit Major, a centre for religious teaching. After a spell on the island of Piro – perhaps Caldey Island – he returned to become Abbot of Llantwit. Many strange events surround this Saint. He was said to have had a dream in which he saw Saints Peter, James and John, and during his service of ordination as a bishop, a dove was seen to hover above his head. It was in Cornwall where he met St Petroc, the latter was standing up to his neck in the waters of any icy hill stream. It was Petroc's habit to torture himself in this manner daily – a flesh-mortifying ritual which lasted from 3 a.m. until cock-crow.

Samson trundled on across Cornwall with his wagon load of books and sacred vessels harnessed to two horses. On Bodmin Moor, he performed a miracle on a boy who had fallen from a horse. He carved a large cross on a stone which local pagans were worshipping, and baptized them. At Golant, where he rested, he destroyed a serpent in a cave. But three fascinating contemporary figures are missing from Samson's biography – King Mark, Queen Iseult (or Isolde) and the knight, Tristan. Their tragic triangular love match was food and drink to every travelling minstrel and troubadour throughout Europe for centuries afterwards and, since Samson knew King Mark, whose palace at Castle Dore was close to Golant, it seems inexplicable that no mention is made of the trio in the biography. But perhaps the writer of the time needed to be discreet.

It is possible, of course, that Samson may have left for Dol, in Brittany, before the lovers met, and was unaware of their tragic love story. Nevertheless, the poet Beroul, who wrote up the epic, sometime during the latter half of the twelfth century, could scarcely fail to mention the name of the great Saint Samson in Tristan and Iseult's unsought and hopeless passion. After all, it added some spice, a touch of the religious to the romantic. Samson died in 565, and his feast day is celebrated on July 28.

ST SIDWELL

As with Boniface, St Sidwell, the gentle virgin daughter of Beorna was of Anglo-Saxon extraction. But it is just possible that she was martyred by Celtic peasants. For all their fearsome onslaught on the Celts, the Anglo-Saxons could not possibly have slaughtered, or driven all the five million inhabitants of Britain to the west. Across the country, where Celts survived, they would doubtless have been used as labourers for the Anglo-Saxons pouring in to settle and farm this fertile land. St Sidwell's beauty was renowned, but there is a Cinderella-like quality to part of her story. She was hated by her wicked stepmother, who conspired, we are told, with a group of peasants.

Various dates are given for St Sidwell's murder. Baring-Gould suggested it was around 560, but others believe it was nearer 700. Whenever, St Sidwell was taking a walk through her father's fields, not far from the city of Exeter's East Gate, when a group of serfs set upon her. They drove a scythe through her neck. Desperately, the conspirators tried to hide the evidence. But a stream of pure water suddenly flowed from the spot where the blood fell from the young virgin's severed head, and a brilliant shaft of light shone out over her body. After three days, so the legend goes, the radiant corpse, its head now rejoined to the torso, walked away to the spot where they built a church to her memory, about 100 yards from the East Gate. The spring of pure water stood, it has been said, next door to a house in Exeter's Well Street.

It is a story which is full of meaningful motifs. Death and transfiguration. The ritual of the corn dolly, and of fertility rites. And, of course, it harks back, in some ways, to ancient Egypt and to Osiris – to the lamentations of the corn god killed by the reapers' sickles. St Sidwell's memory is venerated through wells at Morebath, in North Devon, at Stogursey in Somerset, and at Laneast, in East Cornwall. The relics of Southware, one of St Sidwell's three sisters, were honoured at Sherborne, in Dorset. The Saint herself is invariably depicted beside a stream of pure water, and carrying a scythe, the sharp instrument of her martyrdom.

An old photograph of Exeter Cathedral. It was close by that St Sidwell, a young girl, who was taking a walk through fields, was murdered by serfs around 560.

Profiles of other Saints

St Adwen

Said to be the patron Saint of sweethearts. Lent her name to Advent, near Camelford. One of the daughters of King Brychan. Sometimes referred to as St Anne or St Tane.

St Agnes

Patron Saint of St Agnes. She was not a Celtic Saint, but a beautiful and gifted Roman girl, who was martyred early in the fourth century at the tender age of 13 years. When fire would not consume her, she was executed.

St Allen

The parish lies north of Truro, and St Allen is said to have been a Bishop of Quimper. His name is given as Allun or Alun in the Exeter Episcopal Registers, and his feast day as February 22.

St Anne

Well at Whitstone, with the words St Anna carved into it. Anne, or Ana, was the mother of St Samson, and, therefore, especially esteemed by the Bretons. The name is intertwined and entangled both before and after Christ's birth with the Great Earth Mother.

St Austol

See chapter on Notable Saints. Patron Saint of St Austell; Leland recorded that Austolus was a hermit.

St Barry

Of Fowey. Confusion exists between two Saints, Barry and Finbar. The earliest reference to Fowey, around 1170, describes the church as St Barrianus, but by 1281 it was called St Fymbrianus. In 1464 it became St Fimbari de Fawy. A particularly fine cross in the garden of Menabilly is called Barry's Cross. The Saint drowned off Barry Island.

St Berriona or Beriana

Patron of St Buryan, near Land's End. She was a slim and lovely woman of illustrious birth, and rated a mention in the Exeter Martyrology of Bishop Grand-isson. Her prayers are said to have cured King Geraint's son of a form of paralysis. In art, she is represented as an Irish nun, in white, with a heron, perched upon a tower, at her side.

**St Brigid, Patron Saint of Bridestowe, Devon, possessed a dry sense of
humour, the result of her dealings with lepers no doubt.**

St Blaise

Patron Saint of St Blazey. He was a bishop who was martyred in Armenia in the fourth century. His name is invoked by those who suffer from throat problems.

St Boniface

See chapter of Notable Saints. A name which will always be venerated in his home town of Crediton, as well as throughout Germany, where he converted thousands of heathens.

St Branwalader

Patron Saint of St Breward, whose names means 'Raven Lord'. He is especially famous among the Bretons, and could well have been a companion, or even the successor, of St Samson at Dol. He is also referred to as St Breward, and, by Nicholas Roscarrock as St Brever whose foundation was St Breward or Simonsward. His feast day is in February. St Breward was one of the Cornish parishes whose wealth was drained before the Reformation by the Dean and Chapter of Exeter Cathedral.

St Brannoc

Patron Saint of Braunton. According to Dom John Stephan, OSB., of Buckfast Abbey, St Brannoc arrived at Braunton, in North Devon, complete with his wife, children and tombstone, and set to work on clearing living space in the forest, which he achieved with the aid of wild harts. The good Catholic priest suggests that Brannoc's cult was particularly resistant to Puritan influence! But some argue that Braunton also boasts another Patron Saint, St Brynack – Brychan, perhaps? – and the delightful tradition that the cuckoo is said to send forth its first note on that Saint's Day, April 7.

St Breaca

Breage is the mother church of Cury, Germoe and Gunwalloe, and St Breaca was the virgin Abbess of Killbrig, and a pupil of the great St Brigid. She was said to have come to Cornwall with St Senen who died in 544.

St Brigid

Patron Saint of Bridestowe, in Devon. She is said to have possessed a dry sense of humour, doubtless as a result of her dealings with lepers. Upon her altar, it is said, burns a perpetual fire. She, like another Irish St Berriona, is represented in white habit and veil, with wild geese at her side.

St Brioc

Patron Saint of St Breoke a parish which, Charles Henderson tells us, together with the larger part of the Padstow peninsula, formed the great manor of Polton, or Pawton. It was one of the large and relatively prosperous estates seized by King Egbert around 838 when he defeated the combined Cornish and Viking force. Pawton is unquestionably one of Cornwall's oldest inhabited sites, and seems most likely to have belonged to the monks of St Petroc of Padstow long before Egbert seized it. King Athelstan gave it to the See of Crediton, and from thence it passed to Exeter.

Henderson believed that Pol-ton or Paw-ton had an even earlier name, before the Anglo-Saxon 'Ton' was added. St Brioc, of whom there was a biography written in the eleventh or twelfth century, is said to have learned the rudiments of the Latin language in a day, and the whole book of Psalms, by heart, in five months. Canon Doble, who had a particular affection for this Saint, suggests that there was more literature than history in Brioc's biography! Doble visited Brioc's tomb at St Serge in June, 1928. In ceremonies performed there on May 1, Doble noted, gifts of bouquets of violets were ex–changed, and Mass was followed 'by the wildest revelries!' Brioc, a native of Cardigan, and a friend of **St Tudy** died in Brittany at the monastery he founded, Saint-Brieuc, at the age of 90 in 530. He is the patron Saint of pursemakers, and his feast day is on May 1, which inevitably makes him a popular Saint among the people.

St Budoc

A bishop and confessor, and patron Saint of Budock, Budock Vean in Constantine, Cornwall, and at Budshead and St Budeaux, Plymouth, in Devon and also, possibly, according to local historian Lionel Govier, at Walkhampton, on the edge of Dartmoor. His relics are preserved in the parish church of Plourin, and Budoc's memory is especially cherished on the islands off the tiny port of Paimpol.

He was said to have been born in a cask, at sea, and was given the name Beuzac because he was found in water. He was, possibly, not altogether Celtic, since he seems to have received his pallium, or bishop's cloak, at the hands of Pope Gregory III in Rome, which would make Budoc a contemporary of St Boniface.

St Cadix or St Carroc

There is a small, sequestered inlet on the tidal reaches of the River Fowey, a haunt of heron and mute swans, known as St Cyric's Creek. A graceful old farmhouse, called St Cadix, stands at its head beside a busy stream which slips down through steep meadows past the remains of a holy well in a dell.

St Cadix is believed to be a

distortion of St Carroc. There is fragmentary evidence in stone of an early religious foundation. Carroc himself may have landed here in the Age of the Saints and established an oratory in this secluded hollow. In the Middle Ages, the Saint's name, only half-remembered, became confused with those of St Caradoc, St Cyricus and Cyricus's mother, St Julitta. That this was a hermitage there can be no doubt.

The powerful despot Count Mortain seized this Church land soon after the Conquest, but his son, in atonement, gave it to Montacute Priory in Somerset. A Prior and a monk established themselves here and, by the Dissolution, in 1539, three clerics occupied this hallowed riverside site. Last century, a five-inch high copper relic, a statuette of Christ crucified, was discovered here. Carroc's name is also associated with a holy well at Harlyn Bay.

St Cadoc

Patron of the parish of Padstow, and one of the most important among Welsh saints. A founder of Llancarfan monastery, where such Saints as St Brendan and St Malo received their training. Cadoc travelled widely, to Rome and Jerusalem, and was said to possess special healing powers.

It is from Lifris's life of St Cadoc that we learn that St Michael's Mount was once called Din-sol, from whose hill-fort the Celtic Divinity, of Sol, or Sul (the Sun), was worshipped. Cadoc is remembered at the Holywell Chapel at Harlyn Bay, and his feast day is on September 25.

St Carantoc

The patron Saint of Crantock, whose story is told in the stained glass windows of the beautifully adorned church. Carantoc gave his name to many places in Cornwall, Wales, Brittany and Ireland, and has a reputation as a healer of the blind, the lame and of the mentally sick. Crantock once had a holy well, dedicated to **St Ambrusca,** (or St Ambrose), a name which means strength.

St Clare

Patron of St Cleer. Wilkie Collins wrote of the melancholy decay of poor Clare's Holy Well here: his words helped prompt its restoration. Clare was, perhaps St Clarus, who left her nunnery to escape the unwanted attentions of a nobleman, who eventually murdered her. Feast day is November 4.

St Clare, patron of St Cleer in Cornwall, is remembered by her well in the village.

St Clement

Derived from a Bishop of Rome who was martyred around AD 99.

St Clether

One of the children of King Brychan of Brecknock. The Reverend Sabine Baring-Gould restored the dilapidated well. Clether was surnamed The Aged, and was said to have settled in the Inney Valley beneath the lofty hog's back of Laneast Downs, which cut off the keen Atlantic winds. Later, he moved to St Cleer. Baring-Gould believed that **St Nectan** was Clether's uncle.

St Columb

Nicholas Roscarrock says this patron Saint was forced to flee the attentions of her pagan lover who, nonetheless, found and beheaded her. Columba is a Latin word meaning love.

St Conan sometimes Gonand

Known best as the Patron Saint of the spectacular Roche Rock, and one of the first Bishops of Cornwall. He is also patron of the little church at Washaway.

St Congar

Honoured in Lanivet Parish and a pioneer missionary in the Celtic kingdoms. Associated with **St Clether.** Buried at Congresbury in Somerset where a light burned before his statue right up to the time of the Reformation. Congar was said to have worn a cilicium, an undergarment of goat's hair.

There is a farm about a mile distant from Lanivet Church, called St Ingongar, known, in Armada Year (1588) as St Gonger, which was also the site of a chapel and a holy well. Congar is honoured in Brittany, Anglesey and Somerset. His staff is said to have grown into a yew tree.

St Constantine

Patron Saint of Constantine, and of Milton Abbot, near Tavistock, in Devon. Popular among Christians since he bore the same name as the first Christian Roman Emperor. A king of Dumnonia, that is, Devon and Cornwall, who was not converted, however, until he was 79 years old. Near the church named in his honour on the sand hills in St Merryn Parish, stands a holy well, which was buried until its excavation in 1911. His feast day is on March 9.

Constantine was a Cornishman, son of Padarn, at a time when the Saxons were founding the kingdom of Wessex. It seems that he was concerned in some political scandal, involving the death of two royal children. Following this event, and the loss of his wife, remorse and a spirit of repentance overtook him, and drove him into taking holy orders.

St Corentin or St Cury

Patron Saint of Cury. He was the first Bishop of Quimper. His feast day is on December 12.

St Credan

Patron Saint of ancient Sancreed, near Penzance. Nicholas Roscarrock wrote: 'I have heard that he killed, by misfortune, his own father, with which he was moved as abandoning the world. He became a hogherd and lived so exemplary after, he was esteemed a Saint.' St Credan's aunts, Etaine and Derwe, (which means daughter of the Rowan tree, famed for its ability to drive away witches), were said to have founded churches at Camborne and Sithney. St Credan died in 590.

St Crowan or Crewenna

Patron Saint of Crowan, who built an oratory on the site of the existing church of Crowan around 1,400 years ago. He was said to have come from Ireland with St Breaca and St Senen.

St Cuby

Patron Saint of Tregony and Duloe, and the only Cornish Saint which we definitely know to have been born in Cornwall. It seems that he was son of St Selevan. He travelled to Wales and Ireland before settling in Anglesey, where he is remembered as Cybi Lan – Holy Cybi. His relics were carried off by Irish searovers, or pirates, and eventually found their way to the high altar of Holy Trinity, now Christ Church, Dublin. Cuby was born at Duloe, near Liskeard, though Baring-Gould believes it was in Callington.

Among the tales which surround his life is one concerning a visit to Rome at a time when there was a papal vacancy. As the election was in progress, a dove descended and alighted on this holy Cornishman. He was chosen, by acclaim, to be Pope, but refused the honour, saying he was too simple a man. In his stead, says Baring-Gould, Hilary was chosen. But this could hardly have been feasible, since Hilary was Pope between 461 and 468, and, according to Baring-Gould, Cuby died in 554. Small wonder that Canon Doble was annoyed with some of Baring-Gould's wilder assessments. A Welsh proverb is attributed to the Cornishman Cuby: 'There is no worse misfortune than wickedness.' His feast day is November 8.

St Cuthbert

This patron Saint of St Cubert was once the Abbot of Lindisfarne. His bones were said to have been brought to Holywell.

St David or Dewi

St David or Dewi (462-544) is the patron Saint of Davidstow, or Dewstone. The great Welsh saint is believed to have visited

79

Cornwall, since he was traditionally said to have been an uncle to King Arthur, whose castle of Damelioc was situated only a few miles west of David-stow at Tregeare, near Pendogget in St Kew.

St Day

Patron Saint of St Day, also called St Dei, a Breton. The Saint's name is invoked by those afflicted with rheumatism. His cult is said to have been popular, rather than official.

St Decuman

Venerated at St Degibma, near Helston.

St Dominic and St Indract

Indract, son of an Irish Prince, founded Landrake; St Dominic is venerated in the Tamar Valley, where he and Indract worked and lived together. Their tombs were said to have been placed on either side of the altar of the Old Church at Glastonbury Abbey, until it was destroyed by fire in 1184. William of Malmesbury said Indract was martyred with seven companions near Glastonbury and, at their deaths, a great pillar of light appeared, which sceptics put down to luminous exhalations from nearby marshland. Some say that St Dominic was Indract's sister. Not so, says the authoritative Canon Doble – 'she' was a 'he' – a Saint of this name is the eponym of a parish in Brittany.

St Endelienta

Virgin daughter of King Brychan who settled at Trekenny or Treteny. A chapel on Lundy was dedicated to her. Said to have lived on milk from a cow which the Lord of Treteny killed after it strayed on his land. This patron Saint of St Endellion miraculously revived the animal. To her was written the lines, 'Vouchsafe sweet Saint my Patronesse to be – To pray for him who humbly prayes to thee.' Nicholas Roscarrock

St Erc

Patron Saint of St Erth. A disciple of St Senen with whom he arrived at Hayle. Baptised by St Patrick. Brother of **St Euny or Uny.** There was a chapel to St Ercus at Trevessa in 1403. Died in 512 aged 90. His feast day is October 31.

St Erney

Venerated at St Erney, near St Germans, and at North Hill, east of Bodmin Moor, where he is sometimes referred to as St Terney.

St Ervan

Erbyn, perhaps, in which case he might have been father of **St Seleven.**

An altar tomb in the South Chapel at St Endellion Church which is the shrine of its Patron Saint St Endelienta.

St Euny or Uny

Patron Saint of Lelant and Redruth, and joint patron of Crowan. Said to have been brother of **St Ia** and **St Erc.** Lelant was the centre of his missionary work. William of Worcester wrote of him on his visit to Cornwall. His day is kept on October 31, the Vigil of All Saints. The font of his ruined church at Metherany was taken away and used as a pig trough until the animals feeding from it dropped dead, according to the romantic historian, Hunt. Chapel Euny is near Sancreed where the well was said by Borlase to possess special healing powers. Hunt says that 'On the first three Wednesdays in May, children suffering from mesenteric disease are dipped three times, against the Sun, and dragged three times round the well over the grass in the same direction.'

St Ewe is a saint of whom we know little. The lovely church is a few miles inland from Mevagissey.

St Eval

Disappointingly little is known of this Saint whose name could, however, have become confused with Ervan's or Erc's. Almost certainly one of the band of Irish Saints.

St Ewe

Patron Saint of St Ewe, but in the absence of a written life story, her origins are obscure. Said to have been associated with St Ursula. Feast day is May 2.

St Feock

Patron Saint of Feock. Fiace was a common name in Ireland. Feock is represented in art either with a harp or else with a chariot and horses.

St Fili

Patron Saint of Philleigh on the River Fal and of Filleigh in North Devon. Worked closely with **St Kea.**

St Finbarre or Finbar

Patron Saint of Fowey – but see also **St Barry.** Finbarrus was from Cork. Somewhat mysteriously, the original patron of Fowey may have been **St Corron,** whose monastery was at Langurthow.

St Fingar or St Gwinear

Of Gwinear. An Irish missionary who led a band of Saints who gave their names to parishes between St Ives and Porthleven. His life story was written by Anselm in the thirteenth century, who says that when Gwinear came to Cornwall, King Theodoric killed a companion Saint and decapitated Gwinear, who picked up his head in his hands and walked away with it to a hill. Canon Doble believes there was good reason to suppose that Gwinear and **St Meriadoc** – Camborne – worked together.

St Genny

From St Genesius, a war-weary Roman soldier who became a Divine here.

St Gerant or Geraint

The royal patron Saint of Gerrans. A King of Cornwall who lived during the time of the Yellow Plague (547). The name has been an inspiration for Tennyson's Idylls – he found it in the Mabinogion – and Elgar's Dream of Gerontius – the Romanized spelling. Linked with both the Roseland peninsula and, hopefully, Tintagel.

St German

Patron Saint of St Germans. He lived from 380 until 448. A Gallo-Roman, he was an outstanding administrator, whose fame spread as a result of his opposition to Pelagian heresy. He arrived in England long before St Augustine, and it is to him Christian Celts owe a great debt. Not impossible that he should have sojourned at marvellous St Germans en route for Gaul.

In March, 1358, Sir Nicholas Tamorze gifted two sacred relics, a small arm bone and part of the shroud of St Germans to the cathedral-church at St Germans – items which Nicholas obtained from the Abbot of St German's Convent in Auxerre. But this was an era of massive fraudulence in relics, faked to boost visitor numbers.

St Gluvias

Patron of St Gluvias, Penryn. Had it not been for the destruction of Glasney College at the Reformation Penryn might have become a great Celtic cultural centre. Gluvias was a Welsh Saint, nephew of St Petroc and brother of St Cadoc.

St Goron, Goran or Guron

Honoured at Gorran. A hard-working, holy man, and disciple of

Petroc at Bodmin. His copious spring of water flows into St Guron's Well, Bodmin.

St Gothian

Patron Saint of Gwithian. Traditionally, it is said the Saint was martyred in this area. A chapel to St Gothian is now hidden by sand, but it served as a church and cemetery for a straggling village called Conerton, now overwhelmed by sand. 'Gwithian people are said to have turned-in toes as a result of walking over so much sand' – Charles Thomas. There is an ancient tale of how a flock of sheep, blown by wind into St Ives Bay, were 'caught' by fishermen, who believed them to be a new species!

St Gudwal, Gurval or Gwelvela

Patron Saint of Gulval, whose feast is kept on June 6. Created a breakwater to still the tide and to reclaim land, and was said to have 'walked over the water'. He was of a noble family. The monastery where he died is said to have glowed all night with light when the Saint was buried. A blind man, touching his bier, regained his sight.

St Helen

Honoured at Helland, at Parracombe in North Devon and at Abbotsham. Also a chapel on Lundy. Known as Elen of the Hosts, a British princess, often confused with other Helens.

St Hermes

A Roman martyr remembered at St Erme, St Ervan and Marazion.

St Hieritha

Patron Saint of Chittlehampton, in North Devon. Probably not Celtic.

St Hydroc

The splendid National Trust mansion near Bodmin may conceal in its name a founding monastery to this Saint, since the word Lan, in Cornwall, indicates a place of burial, or holy enclosure.

St Ia or Hya

Of St Ives. Sister of Euny, and a contemporary of Gwinear. She was a Saint with a considerable cult in West Cornwall. St Ives was named in her honour, its ancient name being Porthia. Her feast day is February 3, and her well, situated between the cemetery and Porthmeor, is called Ventonia. She was supposed to have sailed to Cornwall on a leaf.

St Ildierna

Maybe Bishop Hyldren, whose remains were placed in Lansallos Church, between Polperro and Polruan. But the identity of St Ildierna is lost, though Lansallos was, doubtless, a Celtic monastery.

The splendid National Trust mansion near Bodmin, Lanhydrock, may
conceal in its name a founding monastery to St Hydroc.

St Indract

Tamar Valley – but see entry under St Dominic.

St Issey

Patron of St Issey, but known under name Yse, and the Saint appears to have been one of King Brychan's children. Note also Mevag-issey.

St Juliot

Another of King Brychan's brood, honoured at Boscastle. It is also possible that she was the founder of the chapel on the island at Tintagel. The great English writer Thomas Hardy was associated with her namesake church at Boscastle. A name to watch.

St Just-in-Roseland

Ancient name was Lansioch, another link between Cornwall and Brittany. Patron Saint of Lancieux was Simaus or Cieux, and the rock on the cliff where he was martyred is 'stained' red.

St Just

From the name Justin or Yestin – son of the saintly King Gerent or Geraint of Cornwall. See also **St Keverne.**

St Kea and St Fili

Inseparable. Patrons of Kea and Philleigh in Cornwall, Landkey and Filleigh in North Devon. Kea contains the Mal Pas, closely associated with the Tristan-Iseult story. St Ké, or Kenan, was born to rich parentage in Brittany. No Saint, it is said, was a patch on him at curing children's disorders. He was also believed to watch over property. Kea and **St Rumon** may have been Glastonbury-trained.

St Keverne

See chapter on Notable Saints. Patron of St Keverne, which was known as Lanachebran in the Domesday Book.

St Kew and St Docco

Patron of St Kew. His monastery features in the story of **St Samson**, and his followers, who were turned away by the monk, Winnianus, when they sought to visit Docco. Winnianus said the monastery was not ready to receive Samson. Lan-docco was the ancient name of St Kew, it may have been a Welsh colony.

St Keyne

Another of King Brychan's children, who performed miracles through the strength of her purity. Originally, she was patron of not only St Keyne, but also of St Martin's-by-Looe, known as St Kayn juxta Loo. Southey wrote of her well: 'If the husband, of this gifted well, should drink before his wife, a happy man henceforth is he, for he shall be master for life. But if the wife should drink it first, God help the husband then! The stranger stooped to the Well of St Keyne, and drank of the water again.' The Cornishman, who related this tale to the 'stranger' admitted that his wife was wiser than he, for she had carried a bottle of the well-water into church on their wedding day!

St Ludgvan

See chapter on Notable Saints.

St Mabyn

Sister of **St Minver** and **St Endelienta,** and, therefore, a daughter of King Brychan. Nicholas Roscarrock said that a hymn was sung to her signifying that she had 23 brothers and sisters. She died on November 18 about the year 550.

St Madernus

After whom Madron, with its famous well, is named.

St Mawes

Patron of St Mawes. Probably from one of the great monasteries of South Wales. Known as St Maudez in Brittany.

St Mabyn, sister of St Minver and St Endelienta – a daughter of King Brychan. Alice Boyd's photograph shows a window in St Mabyn Church.

St Mawgan

Patron of the Mawgans, in Pydar and Meneage. Nicholas Ross-carrock suggests that he was a Bishop of the Isles of Scilly, in which case both St Mawes, and St Mawgan might be none other than Maudetus, or even Maudernus of Madron fame. Another suggestion is that Mawgan originated from the personal name Malcolm, or Malcant.

St Melanius or Melaine

Patron of Mullion and St Mellion. Melanius, a bishop of Rennes, was a contemporary of St Remigius, a bishop of Rheims, and helped influence Clovis, the powerful King of the Franks. The Mullion feast day is on November 9.

St Melor

Gave his name to Mylor and to Linkinhorne. A Breton or Cornish Prince and martyr, St Melor is mentioned in the life of Melorus. Said to have had his foot and hand replaced by metal as a boy – and they grew as normal!

St Meriadoc

Patron Saint of Camborne, and the subject of a miracle play, Beunans Meriasek. Said to have been a Rohan, born in Pontivy, now – remarkably and coincidentally – twinned with Tavistock (see St Rumon). According to old custom, Camborne people are called Mearageeks, which signified their obstinacy! It was said to be the habit of miners to place a tiny clay image over the first set of timbers to a level, and when that level was begun to call out what sounded like: 'Send for the merry curse and the priest,' which, in Cornish, would have been 'Sen Meryasek, ny a-th-pys' or 'St Meryasek, we pray thee . . .'

St Merryn

Dedication believed to have originated with St Marina, who was born in Bithynia in the eighth century.

St Meubred

Patron of Cardinham, and thought to have been an Irish hermit. Linked in stained glass window of St Neot with St Mabyn.

St Mewan

See **St Austol** and chapter on Notable Saints.

St Michael

Appeared to fishermen at St Michael's Mount on May 8, 495, when the island was home to hermits and anchorites. He has a special role in Cornwall as a guardian. Archangel and Taxiarch of Heaven.

88

St Minver

Also St Mynwer, or My Fair One, or Minwear. Sister to Nectan. Nicholas Roscarrock wrote – 'At her well, the ghostly Adversary coming to molest her as she was combing her hair she, slinging her comb at him, forced him to fly, who left a note behind him to this day Topalundy (Top of Lundy?)' Feast day November 23.

St Mithic or Maidoc

Patron Saint of Falmouth, whose old name was Smithick. In art Mithic is represented as a bishop carrying a hive of bees.

St Morwenna

Of Morwenstow. Died in her brother Nectan's arms gazing across the Severn to her Welsh homeland. She was wise, holy and learned. Her well, repaired by Hawker, is half-way down a cliff.

St Nectan

See chapter on Notable Saints. Eldest of Brychan's children, who are listed as Nectanus, Johannes, Wensent, Endelient, Menfre, Dilie, Tedda, Malem, Wenon, Merwenna, Wenna, Juliana, Yse, Morwenna, Whimp, Weneder, Elender, Kerie, Jona, Kanaunt, Kethender, Adwen, Helie and Tamalant. A life of St Nectan was found in 1937, and among the miracles is the following: 'A certain young man of the house of Oliver de Traci named Vivian, one Summer's day adorned his bed with green herbs and sweet-smelling flowers, and went to sleep thereon at noon. On awakening, he lost both his senses and his memory. In consequence, he wandered about and, in our sight, did many unbefitting things. At last, he came to the relics of the Blessed Martyr Nectan, venerated and kissed them, and was entirely restored to his senses again. We have seen the same happen to a young woman ...' Is there a hint here in the 'green herbs' of the age-old problem of drug-taking, and was Oliver de Traci an ancestor of one of St Thomas à Becket's murderers?

St Neot

See chapter on Notable Saints. Traditionally, St Neot is said to have been a relative of King Alfred The Great.

St Neulina

Patron of Newlyn East. Nicholas Roscarrock said she was a martyred maiden. A Breton Saint of the same name was martyred near Pontivy.

St Nonna, Nona or Non

Mother of St David, said to have been the founder of Bradstone Church, in West Devon.

St Paul Aurelian (St Pol de Leon)

Patron of Paul, also of church at Staverton, Devon. Product of the famous Welsh monastery at Lantwit Major. St Paul of Aurelian's fame reached the notice of King Mark of Cornwall, who wanted to create him a Bishop. But Paul had a dream in which an angel told him to 'tarry no longer in that place'. The Saint asked Mark for a parting gift of seven bells, used to summon guests for meals. Mark refused his request. Paul left for Brittany, and founded a monastery at Ploudalmezeau.

There, he healed the blind, the dumb and those with paralysis. He was also able to calm wild creatures on the Isle of Batz, where he lived. Miraculously, one of the bells he had sought from Mark turned up – in the belly of a huge salmon. His relics, including the bell, are still venerated in the cathedral of St Pol-de-Leon. Paul was said to have lived until he was 104.

St Petroc

A great Apostle of Devon and Cornwall. Honoured in, among other places, Padstow and Bodmin. He was also patron of the lovely Baring-Gould church at Lewtrenchard before 1261, when that church was rebuilt and dedicated to St Peter. He founded a great community at Padstow, before moving to Bodmin, the religious capital of Cornwall down to the end of the Middle Ages. The relic stealer who carried his bones to Brittany in 1177 declared, correctly, that they were those of the chief Saint of Cornwall.

Petroc was also an exceptional administrator and he died at Trerovel, on the way from Nanceventon to Lanwethinoc in June 564. Many wonderful tales are told about this lovable man who, it is said, was even kind to dragons! He originated in Gwent, and belonged to the royal house there. The ivory casket, decorated with Arabic worksmanship, which once contained his bones, was, happily, returned to Bodmin Church in October, 1957. But his bell disappeared shortly before the reign of King Henry I, and was never recovered.

St Piala

The Saint of Phillack, and sister to Uny, Erc and Ia, who came to Hayle (Hevl) from Ireland. She may have been massacred by King Teudrig, whose headquarters was at Riviere, near Phillack Church. Before the Norman Conquest, Phillack formed part of the great estate of Conarditone, later Conerton, which is now covered by sand.

St Piran or Perran

Patron Saint of Cornwall, who features extensively in early

chapters of this book. The Saint of miners. Once, in east Cornwall, Picrous-day, the second Thursday before Christmas Day, was kept as a tinners' holiday, but Piran's feast day is March 5. 'A man of unsteady step and festive appearance was often called a Perraner in Cornwall 200 years ago!' Perran was, after St Michael's Mount and Holy Trinity Chapel at St Day, considered the most popular holy place in Cornwall. It is tragic that his little chapel at Perranzabuloe should have been buried beneath the sands to protect it from, among other things, vandals.

St Rumon

See chapter on Notable Saints. Patron Saint of the Ruans, and of Tavistock.

St Samson

See chapter on Notable Saints. Patron Saint of Golant and South Hill.

St Seleven, Selevan, or Levan

Son, or grandson of King Geraint, and his name, in Cornish or Welsh, is equivalent to Solomon. The favourite walk of this cherished Saint was from Bodellen to Rospletha on to St Levan's rocks, as they are still called, and where, it is said, the grass always grows greener. It is

said he lived his life as a hermit at Porth Chapel, below St Levan Church. Borlase said of his well-water that it was good for relieving toothache and sore eyes.

He also advised people to sleep on the flat stone over the spring, to enable the Saint to exert and dispense his fullest influence and healing power. Seleven's name is to be found in the adjoining parish of St Buryan, at Bosliven, which was, in ancient times, Bos-selevan, or the house of Selevan. It is said that the Saint often rested on the rocks, after fishing, and one day gave them a great blow with his fist. He made a prophecy that 'When with panniers astride, a pack-horse can ride, Through St Leven's stone, The world will be done!'

St Senan

Patron of Sennen, the most westerly Cornish parish. Possibly a link with St Senan of Scattery Island in the Shannon estuary.

St Sidwell

See chapter on Notable Saints.

St Sithney

Patron of Sithney, a softened Cornish form of Sezni. William of Worcester says this Saint was buried in Sithney Church, and that when the weather was poor on his feast day, the cross and banners went around by themselves, without the help of any human agency! Sydney, Australia, owes its name to this Cornish Saint, who could kindle fire and turn water into wine. He died in 529.

It was said that the Almighty revealed to Sithney that he intended making him the patron Saint of girls. 'There's nothing worse on earth than women,' exclaimed the Saint, 'except the Devil. They will be forever plaguing me to get them husbands and fine clothes. I should never get a moment's peace.' 'Then how about being patron Saint of mad dogs?' suggested God. 'That's better,' cried the Saint, 'I'd rather them than women.' Sick dogs are still taken to this chauvinist's well on the Breton foreshore, where he is honoured as St Sezni.

St Sulian

Founder of Luxulyan, which, in spelling, differs only slightly from the Breton place name Lossulien – in 1412, Luxulyan was spelt Lossulyan. St Sulian was born in 530 in Wales, and died in 606 at a lovely place called St-Sulian-sur-Rance near St Malo.

St Teath

Patron of St Teath, and one of King Brychan's dozen daughters. Her sister, Adwen, lived only a few miles distant. She is often referred to as St Tedda, and Nicholas Roscarrock says her feast day was observed on May 1, a day of much revelry in the Cornish Kalendars.

St Tudy

There are two sources for the existence of this Saint, he appears among the written lives – as a friend of St Brioc – and through the place name, St Tudy. He was an active missionary, who founded monasteries on islands and rivers in the north and south of Brittany. Feast day is May 11.

St Veep

St Winnoc's aunt, who is first mentioned as Sanctus Vepus in 1288, and then as Sancta Vepa in 1336. Her feast day is observed on June 16.

St Wenna

Patron of St Wenn, and also of Morval, near Looe. The Saint, also had a chapel at Cheristowe in Hartland Parish. The scholar, Loth, believes that the name Trewenna contains the name Winnow and that St Wenna might be the same as **St Winnow.**

St Willow

Patron of Lanteglos-by-Fowey. Some confusion exists over the exact name, which might be Wyllow or Wylloc. However, he seems to have been born in Ireland 'and was piloted by helpful fish up to Pont Pill, where he established his hermitage.' A more beautiful place for a hermitage could hardly exist anywhere. He was slain by Melyn, and his feast day is on July 7.

St Winnoc

Patron of St Winnow – but see also St Wenna. This delightful corner of Cornwall is bounded by the River Fowey, and sits opposite Castle Dore, said to have been the site of King Mark's Palace, and ancient Lantyan, or Lancien in Beroul's poem about Tristan and Iseult. Winnoc, we learn, wore no other garment than sheared sheepskin. He is said to have founded Wormhout, south of Dunkirk, where he was buried. His liturgical cult is largely confined to Flanders and its adjoining district. His feast day is November 6.

St Teath Church

St Winwaloe

Patron of Gunwalloe and Landewednack, and dedications also at East Portlemouth, Salcombe. The perfect example of the close links between Cornwall and Brittany in the Age of the Saints. Canon Doble says that a visitor to Brittany between the fifth and tenth centuries would have found a great number of small monasteries, presided over by a Bishop, or Abbot. The monastery's founder would have been buried within its grounds, and his or her bell, cross, staff and gospel-book retained on the tomb as holy relics.

In the tenth century, a great disaster befell Brittany, when Norsemen conquered the country and occupied it between 914 and 939. The monks dispersed, taking whatever they could to the interior of France. Devon and Cornwall were, at this time, being anglicized. Winwaloe, angel-like in aspect, always modest and humble, was never seen to sit down in church. He died at a great age. God gathered in the 'ripe corn' and Winwaloe's 'cumbering frame of clay,' quite worn out by his earthly exertions, was received into heavenly glory.

93

Acknowledgements and Thanks

Without the epic standard works, The Saints of Cornwall, by the Reverend Gilbert Doble (pub. Dean and Chapter of Truro Cathedral) and The Lives of British Saints by Sabine Baring-Gould and John Fisher (pub. 1907), it would take a lifetime's study to piece together any definitive account. But there are other writers to whom I am indebted, not least Professor Charles Thomas for his classic Celtic Britain (Thames and Hundson, 1986) and Exploration of a Drowned Landscape (Batsford 1985). Also to Aileen Fox for South West England (Thames and Hudson, 1964); to Frank Delany for The Celts (BBC Publications 1986); to Peter McKenzie for The Christians (SPCK 1988); Lloyd Laing for Late Celtic Britain and Ireland (Methuen 1975); Tobias Churton for The Gnostics (Weidenfeld and Nicolson 1987); for Michael Senior's Myths of Britain (Orbis 1979); for A. L. Rowse's Tudor Cornwall (MacMillan 1969); Butler's Lives of the Saints (Burns and Oates 1985); M and L Quiller-Couch's Ancient and Holy Wells of Cornwall (pub. 1945); T. Taylor's The Celtic Christianity of Cornwall (1916); Catherine Rachel John's The Saints of Celtic Cornwall; Robert Hunt's Popular Romances of the West of England (pub. 1881) and gleanings from Parish Church Magazines, The Federation of Old Cornwall Society's Old Cornwall journals, and from Devon and Cornwall Notes and Queries.

I am also most grateful to Alice Boyd and Ray Bishop for the splendid photographs and to Father Philip Caraman SJ, for pointing the way.

James Mildren

St Morwenna, a famous Welsh Saint who came to North Cornwall. This Church stands in the heart of Hawker Country.

Other Bossiney Titles Include

DARTMOOR IN THE OLD DAYS
By James Mildren. 145 photographs.
James Mildren is an author who is at home in the wilderness of his Dartmoor.
'Lovers of Dartmoor will need no persuasion to obtain a copy. To anybody else, I suggest they give it a try. It may lead to a better understanding of why many people want Dartmoor to remain a wonderful wilderness.'
Keith Whitford, The Western

CASTLES OF DEVON
By James Mildren
James Mildren tours the castles of Devon: Castle Drogo, Lydford, Gidleigh, Okehampton, Dartmouth, Barnstaple and Watermouth are some of the castles featured.
'... a welcome addition to one's collection of Westcountry books. In all 17 castles throughout the county are looked at ...'
Elisabeth Stanbrook
The Dartmoor Magazine

HAWKER'S MORWENSTOW
by Michael Williams
A tour of North Cornwall immortalised by Robert Stephen Hawker who was vicar here for 41 years.

MYSTERIOUS PLACES
by Peter Underwood
Visits locations that 'seem to have been touched by a magic hand'. The man who has been called Britain's No.1 ghost hunter reflects: 'We live in a very mysterious world ...'
'... an insight into some of the more mysterious places in the south west.'
David Elvidge
Launceston & Bude Gazette

MYSTERIES IN THE DEVON LANDSCAPE
by Hilary Wreford & Michael Williams
Outstanding photographs and illuminating text about eerie aspects of Devon. Seen on TSW and Channel 4. Author interviews on DevonAir and BBC Radio Devon.
'... reveals that Devon has more than its share of legends and deep folklore.'
Derek Henderson
North Devon Journal Herald

MY CORNWALL
A personal vision of this Celtic land by Daphne du Maurier, Ronald Duncan, James Turner, Angela du Maurier, Jack Clemo, Denys Val Baker, Colin Wilson, C. C. Vyvyan, Arthur Caddick, Michael Williams and Derek Tangye.
'An ambitious collection of chapters.'
The Times, London

Plus . . .

LEGENDS OF CORNWALL
Sally Jones

LEGENDS OF DEVON
Sally Jones

GREAT HOUSES OF CORNWALL
Jean Stubbs

FESTIVALS OF CORNWALL
Douglas Williams

DAPHNE DU MAURIER COUNTRY
Martyn Shallcross

We shall be pleased to send you our catalogue giving full details of our growing list of titles for Devon, Cornwall, Somerset and Dorset as well as forthcoming publications. If you have difficulty in obtaining our titles, write direct to Bossiney Books, Land's End, St Teath, Bodmin, Cornwall.